EDUCATION AND STATESMANSHIP IN INDIA 1797 TO 1910

EDUCATION AND STATESMANSHIP IN INDIA

1797 TO 1910

H. R. JAMES

M. A., CH. CH., OXFORD

GYAN

Published by

Gyan Publishing House
5, Ansari Road
Daryaganj, New Delhi-110002
Phone: 011-47034999, 9811692060
E-mail: books@gyanbooks.com

Distribution Network
gyanbooks.com
India, USA, Canada, UK, Australia, France

ISBN: 978-81-212-9306-8 (PB)
First Published, 1911

2nd Impression 2023

Printed at: Gyan Press, Delhi.

EDUCATION AND STATESMANSHIP IN INDIA 1797 TO 1910

Author: H. R. JAMES

EDUCATION AND STATESMANSHIP IN INDIA, 1797–1910

EDUCATION AND STATESMANSHIP IN INDIA

1797 TO 1910

BY

H. R. JAMES

M.A., CH. CH., OXFORD

INDIAN EDUCATIONAL SERVICE, PRINCIPAL, PRESIDENCY COLLEGE, CALCUTTA

LONGMANS, GREEN, AND CO.

39 PATERNOSTER ROW, LONDON

NEW YORK, BOMBAY, AND CALCUTTA

1911

"Ne segnes sitis in benefaciendo"

PREFACE

THE slightness of these papers, compared with the magnitude of the subject of which they treat, would have decided me against their separate publication, were it not possible, as I conceive, that even in their present shape, they may serve a useful purpose in helping to a better understanding, so necessary for sound judgment, of educational work in British India. I have at the same time some hope that what I have written may tend to hearten educational workers there, both those in the service of Government and those who are outside Government service, for the difficult and often disappointing task on which they are engaged.

The papers appeared in the Calcutta *Statesman* in January, February, and March of this year, and are published with the concurrence of the proprietors. They are reprinted very nearly as they first appeared. A few corrections have been made, which were necessary, or seemed expedient.

H. R. JAMES.

June 27*th*, 1911

CONTENTS

I

THE NEED FOR A REVIEW

The recent formation of a separate branch of the Home Department of the Government of India to deal specially with education, has given new life to the contention that an entirely new departure is required in our system of education, and in Government policy in regard to it. The contention is not new, it is as old as the endeavour to educate at all in British India; for there were always two parties. It has been gaining strength and insistence for some years past; and the last four years with their painful record of murderous conspiracy and desperate outrage have added to the argument the coercive force of things done and suffered, so that it is not surprising, if any who know educational work in India only by these supposed results, look askance at education itself. The expectation that Government intends on the inauguration of the new department not only to undertake large schemes for the co-ordination and extension of education but to initiate a fundamental change in educational policy, shows that we are, or may be, once more at a dividing of the ways. It is scarcely possible to over-estimate the gravity of such a crisis.

To comprehend the full significance of such a new departure as this expectation indicates, it is necessary to pause and look back; to turn away from the present results of three-quarters of a century of strenuous effort over the building up of an educational system, and go back to the beginning with a mind as open as possible to impartial judgment, to see what was the existing state of things when the obligation to educate was first spoken of, to see why in India it was spoken of at all as a concern for Government; why this was attempted and not that, and how step by step we have come to what we all see and many deplore, at the present time. We shall then be in a position to say with some assurance (for we must inevitably carry into our retrospect the knowledge and foresight which the present gives) whether mistakes have been made, and where, and when; and so come with greater sureness to a consideration of how at this date to rectify what has been done wrongly. Without such preliminary discipline we are only too likely to blunder out of one error into another and add to folly, if folly there has been, too precipitate a repentance. It will be for some of us a dismal result, if we have to confess that we have been wrong from the beginning; that we never should have attempted to introduce into India knowledge, as knowledge has been understood in Europe since the time of Descartes and Bacon; that we never should have founded universities; never have encouraged the study of English literature and European science; that we should have held fast to traditional learning and pre-Copernical science, and have based any more popular education which there was scope for strictly on the vernaculars: that it was bad policy, and folly little short of a crime to introduce the races and peoples of Hindustan to the heights and depths of Western speculation, and to the principles that underlie discovery in natural science. It will be a dismal result: but if it is true, the conclusion must be faced practically, and all well-wishers of education must join the Government of

India (if the decision of the Government of India is to lead the way in such reform) in retracing the steps that have been wrongly taken and in laying anew the foundations that have been falsely laid. A dismal result, certainly, after some four-score years of misdirected effort, if such the conclusion must be. But if it falls out otherwise—and for the purposes of this inquiry at least judgment must be suspended—then it may be agreed that no such retrieving of past errors is called for, but rather we may go on with fresh courage in the endeavour to bring a little nearer accomplishment work begun with honest purpose, and carried on at a great cost of labour and expense. One or other of these conclusions must follow such an historical and critical inquiry as is here proposed, and, whichever conclusion is reached, if any assurance of truth can be reached in a matter of so much intricacy and uncertainty, it must be accepted and followed as a guide. Two things will, I think, be allowed by all who have given consideration to this question that, firstly, it is of boundless importance what direction is given to educational policy at the present time; secondly, that we should accept the arbitrament of facts and reason, and maintain or change the system, according as a fair review of the whole problem shows one or other to be justified. That the latter alternative needs to be very seriously taken account of must be admitted when, not to speak of the gathering volume of criticism in India, so friendly and disinterested an observer from overseas as Sir Henry Craik is found endorsing without hesitation the opinion that educational work in India is in its main lines hopelessly wrong.[1]

[1] Sir Henry Craik, "Impressions of India" (Macmillan, 1908), p. 199; cf. pp. 203, 204.

I propose, then, in a series of papers to consider, first, the state of education and learning in India at the time when the movement began, of which the existing educational system is the outcome; next, the first stirrings of the new movement for education. On this it follows to examine in order the successive turning points in the development of the system; the definite adoption of English as the instrument of higher instruction; the formation of education departments; the foundation of universities; the Commission of 1882 together with the great expansion of collegiate education between 1880 and 1900. The growing distrust of the results of this expansion must then be traced till it culminates in the reform of the universities in 1906. This done, it will be well to take up the inquiry on the political side with a view to determining with exactitude the relation of the political to the educational movement: the aspirations of the educated classes must be fairly weighed and estimated, and those that are legitimate distinguished from those that must be summarily condemned: the tendency to resort to violence in furtherance of revolutionary aims must be faced, and the question must be answered whether this tendency is strengthened or opposed by educational influences. Finally, it should be possible to gauge how far the declared educational policy of the present time accords with the conclusions reached and whether any decisive change of aim is called for.

It may confidently be expected that some advantage must result from such a careful and dispassionate examination of the course of educational progress in India. The random judgments of the market-place cannot be trusted. Misconceptions arise from want of information and from want of reflection. There is much current ignorance and much confusion of thought on this subject of education. If the facts of its history can be brought into clearer light, and if more deliberate and more consecutive thinking is given to them, the probability of wrong judgment on the great questions involved is lessened. The issues are momentous. Time given to their consideration should not be grudged.

An additional reason for undertaking the inquiry here suggested may be found in the papers on "Indian Unrest" which appeared last year in the columns of *The Times*, and deservedly attracted close attention both in India and in England.[1] Mr. Chirol's references to education are characterized by moderation and sympathy, but they are not founded on intimate personal experience, nor is it likely he would claim to have made independent inquiry into the early history and progress of the educational movement. The inquiry here proposed is a needed supplement to the discerning analysis of political unrest made in his papers. Mr. Chirol started upon an investigation of political unrest as his main subject of inquiry and is incidentally led to pronouncements on education, because the education given in Indian schools and universities is so manifestly a factor in his problem. Here education will be the main theme; the political effects will be subsidiary. The conclusion reached by these opposite paths and from contrasted starting points may well be widely different. They can hardly be expected to harmonise at all points. If, however, they are found in any particulars to coincide, the probability that here at least we reach firm and solid ground will be reasonably strengthened.

[1] "Indian Unrest," by Valentine Chirol. A reprint, revised and enlarged, from *The Times*, with an introduction by Sir Alfred Lyall. Macmillan, 1910.

II

ORIGIN OF THE EDUCATIONAL MOVEMENT

It is generally admitted nowadays that in order to form a competent judgment of what a thing is, one must know how it arose. We shall certainly be in a better position to form a just estimate of the system of education which has been built up under the tutelage of government in British India, if we examine with some attention the circumstances of its origin. British rule itself was a haphazard, unpremeditated thing. The giving or withholding of education was no part of the plans of Clive, the first founder of the Empire, any more than it was part of the plans of the enterprising Englishmen who formed the Company of Merchants of London trading into the East Indies in the reign of Queen Elizabeth.

Now, whatever may have been the strength and weakness of the Moghul administration in its most flourishing times (and there is no probability that even in the days of Akbar such notions as education and national improvement in the popular sense were ever so much as spoken of), there can be no question that the collapse of that administration brought with it moral chaos and the ruin of learning. The history of the acquisition of power in Bengal by the English is witness enough to the moral anarchy. The strong men whose force of character bore them to dominion out of the welter of struggling interests were tainted by the prevailing corruption. Clive and Hastings are great names, but they are not stainless; though Warren Hastings might well be deemed an angel of light by comparison with some of tho odious desecrators of human character with whom he contended, and Clive a knight as free of reproach as he was undoubtedly free of fear. The whole story of the rise of the political ascendancy of the British in Bengal is ill-reading to one who desires to view in it an edifying spectacle of magnanimity and beneficence: its interest is absorbing to the student of history who sees moral energy latent in the struggles of force and craft. This is where the critic mistakes who in these days turns back and applies the more refined standards of a political morality untried by anything fiercer than Boycott and Press laws to a period of tumultuous conflict, where unscrupulous force carried all that trickery did not filch away. There was neither law nor morality nor enlightenment in the break-up of the Moghul Empire; and the establishment of the Company's authority at first only restored the outward order which is the first condition of their possibility. The rule of the Company was not in its beginning founded on abstract justice and the benefit of the governed. Those ideas were not far distant, because men carry with them to every clime under heaven the ideas of their race and time, and the mere exploiting of Bengal for commercial purposes could not long endure in its integrity. Accordingly before the close of the eighteenth century we find that men's minds were turning already towards the perception of a duty to the millions of men who had so strangely become subjects to a trading company. Clive himself, though not an exponent of the religious and moral ideals of his time, saw this, as his measures on his return to India in 1765 show. He endeavoured to curb rapacity and to lay the foundations of tolerable government; and these are at least the negative conditions which must be secured before active beneficence is possible. Warren Hastings did much more. Whatever his faults, and they have been grossly exaggerated, he was in the truest sense an enlightened and far-seeing statesman; and he it was who, first of Englishmen in India, turned his attention to education. He founded and endowed the Calcutta Madrasa. The nature and purpose of this foundation is significant; but still more significant is it that Hastings recognized the duty of a civilized government to promote education.

That science and learning, both Hindu and Mahomedan, had fallen into a miserable state of decay is plain most of all from the absence of all notice of them in the history of those times. It is only somewhat later, in the opening decades of the nineteenth century, that this lamentable decay is actually described. But the absence of all mention is more eloquent than any notice could be. When Lord Minto in 1811 publicly animadverted on this decay, the fact was itself evidence of a reviving interest. The utter absence of mention in a period of wars, insurrections, treacheries, rivalries, and unscrupulous competition for power, is evidence that there was not interest enough in literature and learning to voice itself in lamentation. In 1811 the first Lord Minto wrote to the Directors: "It is a common remark that science and literature are in a progressive state of decay among the natives of India. From every inquiry I have been enabled to make on this interesting subject, that remark appears to me but too well-founded. The number of the learned is not only diminished, but the circle of learning, even among those who still devote themselves to it, appears to be considerably constricted, the abstract sciences are abandoned, polite literature neglected, and no branch of learning cultivated but what is connected with the peculiar religious doctrines of the people." This neglect may have been partly due to the half-century of rule of a government without spontaneous interest in Oriental literature. But this was not the whole cause, nor is there any ground for supposing that literature and learning were flourishing in Northern India when Clive procured for the Company the Dewani of Bengal, Behar, and Orissa. All the evidence tends to show the contrary. Finally, if one looks back once more to the lamentable history of Hindustan during the whole period of the disruption of the Moghul power, sufficient reason is found a hundred years earlier for the decline of learning which reached its lowest point with the close of the eighteenth century. "The condition of India during the half-century following the death of Aurangzeb may be summed up in one word—misery. . . . After the great emperor had passed away, hell was let loose and the people were ground to the dust by selfish nobles, greedy officials, and plundering armies. Hardly any one appears who is worthy of remembrance for his own sake and there is nothing to be said about literature or art."

The social and political conditions for five hundred years earlier had not been such as to promote the highest ideals of public conduct or foster the manlier qualities of private character. Where had there been room for civic ideals like those of republican Rome, or for the ideas of a law above kings and of personal freedom and responsibility, such as were developed in Europe in the fourteenth century and gradually worked themselves out in English and European history? The first thirty years of British administration did little or nothing to breathe new life into ancient ideals, or introduce new ideals from beyond

Hindustan. No wonder when men, in whom the Christian impulse towards active beneficence and an interest in the uplifting of human character were strong, looked around them, they were impressed—in shocking contrast with the reports of early travellers—by the manifestation on every side of a low state of morality; the absence of truth and trust, the almost universal prevalence of sordid motives, and of a mean self-seeking against which no considerations of right and honour weighed. The first Englishman who gave public expression to a sense of the duty of finding a remedy for this low state of public morality was Charles Grant, a member of the Court of Directors of the East India Company. In 1797 Grant laid before the Court his *Observations on the state of Society among the Asiatic subjects of Great Britain.* His description bears the stamp of simplicity and sincerity. It is inspired by goodwill. It is based on personal experience, as the writer had himself spent many years in India and a considerable time in the interior of the country. It represents the people of India, both Hindus and Mahomedans, in a sadly demoralized state. "Upon the whole," he sums up, "we cannot avoid recognizing in the people of Hindustan a race of men lamentably degenerate and base, retaining but a feeble sense of moral obligation, yet obstinate in their disregard of what they know to be right, governed by malevolent and licentious passions, strongly exemplifying the effects produced on society by great and general corruption of manners, and sunk in misery by their vices, in a country peculiarly calculated by its natural advantages to promote the happiness of its inhabitants." His object was to find a remedy. The remedy he suggested was education and practically what has since been known as English education.

Grant's paper was carefully debated in the Court of Directors, and there was at one time a prospect of the adoption of the measures he advocated. If they had been adopted, the public organization of education in Bengal would have been antedated by nearly half a century. There was opposition, however, and the opposition prevailed. In the end nothing was done. Nevertheless, the question had been raised, the aspiration had been expressed, and Charles Grant deserves to be remembered as the man who first foresaw the possibility of the enlightenment which has since become in India a reality.

III

THE FIRST STIRRINGS

THOUGH no obvious effect followed Charles Grant's endeavour to rouse interest in the obligation of the East India Company, in its ruling capacity, to educate, the idea lived and worked. It is never the man who voices an idea who is the real source of its energy. It comes from without and possesses him. It speaks through him and gains new efficacy from his voice. But the idea—whether of the Baconian philosophy or of negro emancipation—is greater than the man and independent of him. It works on silently when his voice is still, and his message perhaps seems to have been uttered in vain. So the idea of a duty on the part of the British Government to educate and elevate the peoples of India quietly did its work, and in due time was carried into action. But its first results were a quickening of the sense of responsibility to the indigenous learning of the country. Warren Hastings had founded the Calcutta Madrasa in 1781, which is thus the earliest educational institution due to British influence. In 1791 Jonathan Duncan founded a Sanskrit College at Benares, and Government supported the institution with substantial grants. This direction of energy was strongly reinforced by the newly awakened interest in Oriental studies which followed the researches of Sir William Jones and the foundation in 1784 of the Asiatic Society of Bengal. This may, till the time of Macaulay, be said to have been the Government policy in education—that is the revival and encouragement of Sanskrit and Arabic learning; and this was an attempt to continue the traditional policy of preceding administrations, so far as they can be said to have had any conscious policy. Lord Minto's Minute of 1811, quoted in the preceding paper, sufficiently indicates the aim and scope of this policy. The effect of Lord Minto's representation was that in 1813, under Parliamentary pressure, it was directed that not less than a lakh of rupees should year by year be set apart for educational purposes. The actual words of the despatch were "set apart and applied to the revival and improvement of literature, and to the encouragement of the learned natives of India, and for the introduction and promotion of a knowledge of the sciences in the British territories of India." The practical interpretation given to these instructions—whatever may have been in the minds of the framers of the despatch, and this was later to be hotly debated—was that the money was expended in printing Sanskrit and Arabic works, and in paying stipends to teachers and students. Even this was not till 1823, when a Committee of Public Instruction was first formed. Meanwhile, two other factors had come into operation, which anticipated Government in giving quite other directions to educational enterprise. These were, firstly, Christian missionaries; and, secondly, a spontaneous demand for liberal education on the part of some more advanced-thinking members of the Hindu community in Calcutta.

The aims of the missionaries were naturally directed to using education, not as an end in itself, but as a means to evangelization. But the desire to educate as a means to conversion led then, as it has done ever since, to single-minded and whole-hearted labours in the cause of education in and for itself. The culmination is the Scottish Churches College in Calcutta, and the Madras Christian College. The most significant date in these early times is the foundation of the Serampore College in 1818; but Carey, Marshman, and Ward had started English schools earlier in the century. Missionary efforts took a similar direction in Bombay and Madras at about the same time; in Bombay somewhat later, in Madras a little earlier. If this effort had depended for its motive force on religious interest only, it would have accomplished very little. It was powerfully supported, however, by the third factor, a new-found desire on the part of natives of India for a share in the knowledge and training which they discerned to be a large part of the secret of the superior efficiency of nations from the West, and the source of what was strong and admirable in English character. Naturally, the first stirrings of this impulse remain somewhat obscure. They first took solid and tangible shape in the establishment of the Hindu College in Calcutta. The history of that establishment can be told; and, as the history of the Hindu College links itself in the fulness of time with the foundation of Presidency College, Calcutta, and the organization of education departments in all the provinces of British India, we are in that history relating also the substantial beginnings of the movement for education, which has steadily progressed from that day to the present time.

Three names are specially associated with the foundation of the Hindu College: Raja Ram Mohan Roy, David Hare, and Sir Edward Hyde East, and each has some title to greatness. Raja Ram Mohan Roy incarnates the impulse which led thinking Indians to desire and work for "English education." He was an English-educated Bengali before the era of English education. He learnt English before there were English schools, left a considerable literary product written in English, and lies buried in English soil near Bristol. He, more than any man of Indian race, advocated the necessity of a new departure in education; of a new departure in which the ideas and science of the West should liberate the minds of his countrymen and bring new light. He himself broke free from the prejudices and superstitions of the past, and founded a pure theistic form of Hinduism which continues in the three branches of the Brahma Samaj. When it was first proposed to found the Sanskrit College, Calcutta, Ram Mohan Roy raised his voice in protest, and begged rather for the foundation of a modern place of education on the lines of the later founded Arts Colleges. To Ram Mohan Roy, more than to any other, must be ascribed the inception of the project for the Hindu College; but he found a valuable ally in David Hare. David Hare represents the purely philanthropic sympathy which really is sometimes found in European communities for the welfare of the peoples of India. He was not a Government official; neither was he a Christian missionary. Indeed, the independence of his religious views was the occasion for the denial to his dead body of the rites of Christian burial. Wherefore his remains lie to this day under the monument erected by a people's love to his memory, on the south side of the tank in College Square, and within sight of College Street. David Hare had, since his coming to India in 1800, become convinced of the necessity of liberal education for the people of India, and he warmly co-operated with Ram Mohan Roy in the scheme for a college.

Sir Edward Hyde East was Chief Judge of the Supreme Court, and he represents the friendly attitude of the Indian Bench towards education, and that countenance from official society, which has hitherto been thought almost indispensable to the success of any new undertaking. The Chief Justice gave his cordial support. A meeting of leading Hindus was convened in his house; subscriptions were promised, and a Managing Committee was formed. Raja Ram Mohan Roy, though the undertaking was due to his inspiration, was not of the number. His defiance of convention had incurred the resentment of his fellow-countrymen, and when his name proved a cause of offence he voluntarily withdrew it.

The Hindu College was opened January 20, 1817.

IV

THE ADOPTION OF ENGLISH EDUCATION

The declared object of the foundation of the Hindu College was "to instruct the sons of Hindus in the European and Asiatic languages and sciences," and we are told that the first place in importance was assigned to English. The subscribers were mainly Hindus; but there were European subscribers also, Sir Edward Hyde East, Bishop Middleton, Mr. Baretto the banker, and a few others. The original fund amounted to Rs.1,13,179. Instruction in the first years was free and the number of pupils was limited to a hundred. The management was for a time exclusively Hindu. The teaching staff was Indian, and the board of control was Indian. Then, as has happened so often since, difficulties arose, Government aid was solicited, and this aid was given on condition that the college should be open to inspection by Government. This was in 1824. The Government contribution in 1825 was Rs.24,000. A proposal that lectures should be delivered by English professors was made in 1825. Such lectures were first given in 1827, and rather unexpectedly, the subject was medicine: lectures in law were added in 1832. In 1834 Captain Richardson, a young officer of the Bengal army, with a strong bent for literature, and recently invalided from military service, was made Principal. By this time numbers had greatly increased;

the limit of a hundred had been abolished in 1825, and fees were introduced. In 1835 there were 384 students. This was the year of Macaulay's Minute and of Lord William Bentinck's Resolution adopting the encouragement of English education as Government policy.

It has become almost an accepted dictum that we owe English education as it has since been developed all over India to Lord Macaulay. There is some truth in this ascription, but it is already plain that a good deal of qualification is required. A college for giving Hindus an education based on a knowledge of English already existed in 1834 when Macaulay came to India, and in 1835 when he wrote his Minute there were nearly four hundred students in this college. There were also several schools in Calcutta in which English was taught. In 1819 the Calcutta School Society had been founded with the express object of establishing schools; one of the schools thus established being the Arpooly Pathsala developed later into the Hare School. In 1824 a Committee of Public Instruction had been formed in tardy fulfilment of the instructions issued in consequence of Lord Minto's representation of 1811. The reports of the Committee begin regularly from the year 1831. All this shows that organized instruction on modern lines and the beginnings of liberal education in Bengal must be dated from 1816 rather than from 1835.

The position reached in Madras and Bombay was similar but less advanced as regards the study of English. The beginnings of liberal education in each are associated with a name truly great. In Bombay Mountstuart Elphinstone, among his other labours for the public good, interested himself in education. He left India in 1827. A Bombay Education Society had been formed in

1815, and a Bombay Native School Book and School Society in 1822, but there was no institution comparable to the Hindu College in Calcutta. In the year of Elphinstone's departure, however, it was resolved by the principal native gentlemen of Bombay to honour his name by the foundation of Professorships "to be held by gentlemen from Great Britain until the happy period when natives shall be fully competent to hold them." The object of the professorships was the same as that of the Hindu College, Calcutta. This Elphinstone Professorship fund reached a total of Rs.2,15,000. The professorships were duly founded, the first professors, Messrs. Harkness and Orlebar arriving in 1835. As there was no college as yet, the first lectures were given in a room in the Town Hall. The fund and the professorships have ultimately been merged in the Elphinstone College, the Presidency College of Bombay. In Madras Sir Thomas Munro was the first Governor to promote education. In 1822 he instituted an inquiry into the actual state of indigenous education. In 1826 a Board of Public Instruction was formed. Its first efforts were for the improvement of vernacular education, and it was not till 1841 that a High School was opened by Government as part of a scheme for a Madras University. Meanwhile, in 1837, a missionary school had been started, destined to be well known later as the Madras Christian College.

It would appear then that English education was already an existing institution in Bengal and Bombay in 1835, and was on the way to institution in Madras. The glory or infamy of introducing modern education into India is therefore not Macaulay's. When he arrived in India the Hindu College was working in Calcutta on the lines since known as English education, the Elphinstone

Institution in Bombay, and schemes for institutions on the same model in Madras were ripening. Nevertheless, Macaulay's influence as a determining factor in the fortunes of this English education was very great, and the part assigned to him in popular estimation is to a large extent justified. He did decisively determine the inclination of State influence to the side of English education.

Macaulay landed at Madras in June, 1834. Early in October he was in Calcutta. He was appointed President of the Committee of Public Instruction in December, but did not at once take up the duties of the office. Matters on the Committee had at this time come to a strange pass. There had long been differences of opinion on the question of the aim that should guide its operations and a division into two parties: a conservative party upholding the policy of encouraging Oriental literature and a forward party believing it to be possible to introduce a more useful kind of education through the medium of English. This difference of opinion was in practice a contention over the expenditure of the lakh of rupees, which since 1823 had been set aside for educational purposes. The conservative Orientalists were for continuing to devote this sum entirely to the printing of Sanskrit and Arabic books and the payment of stipends. The innovating Occidentalists were for diverting at least a part of it to English education. At the date of Macaulay's arrival the work of the Committee had long been at a standstill. The Committee numbered ten; the two parties on it were nicely balanced, five against five; practically nothing at all could be done. Macaulay refused to take any active part in the business till the dispute was authoritatively settled. In January, 1835, the rival pleas of the two parties were submitted to the

Governor-General's Council for decision, and Macaulay as a member of that Council recorded his opinion in the Minute which has become famous. The precise question which came before Council was whether there was in the terms of the Act of 1813 any legal bar to the use of the educational grant for any other purpose than the revival of Sanskrit and Arabic learning. Macaulay had no difficulty in showing that no such limitation existed by quotation of the text of the Act, which, along with "the revival and promotion of literature and the encouragement of learned natives," enjoins "the introduction and promotion of a knowledge of the sciences." It was clear that the use of part of the funds for new experiments in education was not contrary to the Act but actually prescribed by it, and that no new legislative act was necessary (as had been contended) before funds could be diverted to English. But Macaulay went far beyond this, and wrote a most trenchant statement of the case for a modern course of study as against the antiquated classical learning hitherto maintained by the Committee. That statement is characterized by all Macaulay's absoluteness of diction and some of his particular assertions are indefensible. The point of real importance is, whether he was right in his main contention that the study of English was more useful as the means of intellectual improvement for the classes of India to whom higher education was open than Arabic and Sanskrit. The thesis he proposes for discussion is, "We have a fund to be employed as Government shall direct for the intellectual improvement of the people of this country. The simple question is, what is the most useful way of employing it." He first puts aside the vernaculars on the ground of general agreement that "the dialects commonly spoken among the natives of this part of India contain neither literary nor scientific information, and are, moreover, so poor and rude that, until they are enriched from some other quarter, it will not be easy to translate any valuable work into them." "It seems," he says, "to be admitted on all sides, that the intellectual improvement of those classes of the people who have the means of pursuing higher studies can at present be effected only by means of some language not vernacular amongst them." He goes on, "What then shall that language be? One-half of the Committee maintain that it should be English. The other half strongly recommend the Arabic and Sanskrit. The whole question seems to me to be which language is the best worth knowing."

Macaulay has no difficulty in showing (1) that English is the key to more useful knowledge than Sanskrit or Arabic; (2) that there was already an effective demand for English, whereas the study of Sanskrit and Arabic could only be kept up artificially by the award of stipends; (3) that many natives of India in Calcutta had already a remarkable command of English, so that there could be no doubt of their being able to master English sufficiently for the purpose in view. In his own words, "To sum up what I have said, I think it clear that we are not fettered by the Act of Parliament of 1813; that we are not fettered by any pledge expressed or implied; that we are free to employ our funds as we choose; that we ought to employ them in teaching what is best worth knowing; that English is better worth knowing than Sanskrit or Arabic; that the natives are desirous to be taught English, and are not desirous to be taught Sanskrit or Arabic; that neither as the language of law, nor as the language of religion, has the Sanskrit or Arabic any peculiar claim to our engagement, that it is possible to make natives of this country good English scholars, and that to this end our efforts ought to be directed."

Macaulay's energetic rhetoric was decisive. His Minute is dated the 2nd of February. On March the 7th came the Resolution of the Governor-General: "His Lordship in Council is of opinion that the great object of the British Government ought to be the promotion of European literature and science among the natives of India, and that all the funds appropriated for the purposes of education would be best employed on English education alone."

It was almost Lord William Bentinck's last public act, as he left India on March the 20th, within a fortnight of the date of the Resolution. It is also fair to note that the actual decision, whatever its wisdom, was his rather than Macaulay's, and that Lord William Bentinck's sympathies had been with English education before Macaulay's arrival. Undoubtedly this was a turning point of the very greatest importance; for from that time forward to the present the promotion of liberal education by means of English has been the acknowledged, though by no means the exclusive, aim of the Government educational policy. The battle was fought and decided in Bengal; but its effect was universal in range. Thus Mr. Satthianadhan in appending the text of Macaulay's Minute to his History of Education in the Madras Presidency notes: "This Minute and the following Resolution have been entered here, as having set at rest the question—at the time they were written an important one—as to what should be the character of the instruction imparted in the Government schools and colleges, whether Oriental or European. It is a question which was never raised in Madras, but the decision of which was equally important to this Presidency as to Bengal, for if the advocates of Oriental instruction had carried their point, the Oriental system would probably have been adopted all over India."

V

THE ADOPTION OF ENGLISH—WAS IT A MISTAKE?

The formal adoption of English education as the prime object of Government encouragement was a decision pregnant with important consequences, some of them foreseen and desired; others, though they might have been foreseen and were by some few predicted, would certainly not have been desired. We now know a great deal more of this English education, its possibilities and tendencies; for we have seen its expansion and its results in the seventy-five years which have passed since Macaulay wrote his Minute with such vigour and confidence. It has now to be asked not so much, do we approve the results, as must we still endorse the decision then made: if we were back at that fateful turning-point, would we decide in the same way again?

Some admissions unfavourable to Macaulay must first be made. There was much which Macaulay did not see. He did not see the full necessity of giving attention to vernacular education, though he did not altogether ignore it. He did not see that there might in India be other reasons for the study of Arabic and Sanskrit after the traditional method than the strictly utilitarian. He did not see the necessity of making provision for more than the intellectual side of education. He did not take account of the disintegrating effect of the new truth which he prized so highly, nor had he Plato's perception of the possible value of beneficent falsehood. He had not the imaginative insight or sympathy which would have put him in a right attitude to his subject. He never got into the right relation to India and the East. His pronouncements are too glib, too confident, too unqualified, and sometimes err against good taste. These defects and faults do not alter the real issue, which is, was he right on the main question? Quite apart from Macaulay and his Minute was it right to introduce into India the literature of Europe and modern science? Was it possible to take any other course in view of the question which had arisen; a question which was something wider than the dispute dividing the Committee of Public Instruction. It was the question of the admission, or refusal of admission, to Western enlightenment of the peoples of India, when they asked for it, and when their political history had brought them within its gates. Herein lay the real strength of Macaulay's position and of those who thought with him: "We are withholding from them," he wrote, "the learning for which they are craving; we are forcing on them the mock learning which they nauseate." That this was essentially true is shown by the fact of the establishment of the Hindu College and of the schools which fed it. It was shown also by the actual acquirement of English by natives of India. "There are in this very town," says Macaulay, "natives who are quite competent to discuss political or scientific questions with fluency and precision in the English language. I have heard the very question on which I am now writing discussed by native gentlemen with a liberality and an intelligence which would do credit to any member of the Committee of Public Instruction." This is significant testimony. The true issue had been forcibly stated by Ram Mohan Roy in 1823, the year of the formation of the first Committee of Public Instruction. When the proposal to found a Sanskrit College in Calcutta was put forward, Ram Mohan Roy addressed to Lord Amherst a protest which anticipates Macaulay by twelve years. "We find," he wrote, "that the Government are establishing a Sanskrit school under Hindu Pandits to impart such knowledge as is already current in India. This seminary (similar in character to those which existed in Europe before the time of Lord Bacon) can only be expected to load the minds of youth with grammatical niceties and metaphysical distinctions of little or no practical use to the possessor or to society. The pupils will there acquire what was known 2000 years ago, with the addition of vain and empty subtleties since produced by speculative men, such as is already taught in all parts of India. In order to enable your Lordship to appreciate the utility of encouraging such imaginary learning as above characterized, I beg your Lordship will be pleased to compare the state of science and literature in Europe before the time of Lord Bacon with the progress of knowledge made since he wrote. If it had been intended to keep the British nation in ignorance of real knowledge, the Baconian philosophy would not have been allowed to displace the system of the schoolmen, which was the best calculated to perpetuate ignorance. In the same manner the Sanskrit system of education would be the best calculated to keep this country in darkness, if such had been the policy of the British Legislature." He goes on, "But as the improvement of the native population is the object of Government, it will consequently promote a more liberal system of instruction; embracing mathematics, natural philosophy, chemistry, anatomy, with other useful sciences which may be accomplished with the sum proposed, by employing a few gentlemen of talents and learning, educated in Europe, and providing a college with the necessary books, instruments, and other appliances."

This appeal is unanswerable. The British people having—through whatever accidents and by whatever means—come to bear sway in Bengal and other parts of India, they could not wilfully and deliberately shut out from India the light and science in which they themselves had been nurtured. It was inevitable what the answer must be when the question was asked in a plain and definite way, which there was no shirking, whether by Ram Mohan Roy, or by Thomas Babington Macaulay. The answer had to be "We will admit this light." "We will help forward the enlightenment to the utmost extent of our resources." The question has been asked again virtually at every crisis of the history of education in India, and though there have always, it must be acknowledged, been dissentients, and competent dissentients, the verdict of thoughtful and far-seeing statesmanship, as represented by the most highminded and the most authoritative administrators, has always been the same.

The obligation to forward enlightenment being admitted, the use of English as the instrument follows of practical necessity, and English education with its methods and implications is the result. There is one further most potent consideration. English education would have come independently of Lord William Bentinck's decision. It would have come in somewhat different garb, and its progress would have been slower; but it would have come. When day has dawned you cannot shut out the light by merely refusing to open the windows. It streams in through every crevice and cranny, and knowledge is even more penetrative than daylight;

for, when the windows are shut, it percolates through them. This is proved sufficiently, I think, by the existence in 1835 of the Hindu College and the success it had obtained, not, it is true, altogether without Government aid, yet mainly through forces independent of Government. It is proved by the use made of English in controversy by Ram Mohan Roy, and by the germination of new thought which his religious activities showed. If Government had systematically opposed instead of systematically promoting the vitalizing thought of the West, the educational advance might have been delayed; but there is every probability that it would have come eventually. Japan, Persia, China, Turkey, all give witness in different fashions and in varying degrees to that probability. How exactly it would have come and with what force, and how far the effects would have been identical with, or would have differed from, those we are familiar with, it is impossible to say with certainty, but there is a possibility that the ultimate force would not have been less, and that the disintegrating tendency would have been stronger than has actually happened.

When the question of Macaulay's time is fairly faced again with a perception of what the circumstances then were, and a recognition of what the actual results have been, the conclusion is almost inevitable that the answer found was the only answer possible. Modern education through English had to come, if British rule continued—or even if it did not—and it was better that it came as it did with the approbation and under the control of Government than as an intrusive and almost clandestine thing, under suspicion from the authorities, if not positively forbidden. The advent of the English as rulers in Bengal meant the advent of English ideas and English literature, and the mere force of imitation and emulation brought about that the more forward spirits among the natives of India aspired to gain the more advanced knowledge of Europe, and to breathe the freer air of European thought. The ideas could not be kept out because the English brought them with them, and exhaled them in their speech and conduct. It was inevitable that these ideas should germinate and take root in the surrounding soil: they belong to the spirit of the time. They were all-pervading, and would have entered without doors. It was more prudent as well as more generous to help to introduce what could by no precautions have been kept out. It was more politic, though it is not to be supposed that such prudence was the motive from which the pioneers of English education acted. The spirit of the movement for the promotion of the new education is faithfully expressed by men like Sir Thomas Munro and Mountstuart Elphinstone. It is they, and not Macaulay, who were the true initiators of English education.

Too much significance cannot well be ascribed to this turning-point; for all that follows is contained within it by implication. Possibly Charles Trevelyan did not really overstate the matter when he wrote: "So much, perhaps, never depended upon the determination of any Government."[1]

[1] Trevelyan, "On the Education of the People of India," 1838, p. 12.

VI

PROGRESS 1835 *TO* 1854

A MARKED invigoration of educational activity in Bengal followed Macaulay's accession to the Committee of Public Instruction. It is possible that English education owes more to his organizing industry than to his Minute. At the beginning of 1835 there were fourteen institutions under the control of the Committee. Seven new institutions were started during 1835 and six more were in process of establishment. By the end of 1837 there were forty-eight institutions with 5196 pupils, of whom 3729 were in Anglo-Vernacular schools or colleges. The average monthly expenditure was Rs.25,439. These figures are by present standards moderate enough, but they show a great advance on 1835: they show also how largely educational effort in Bengal was at this time expended on English education. Progress continued steadily from year to year on these lines. An extensive system of scholarships was introduced in 1839 and added a new motive to exertion. In 1852 the number of scholarships in Bengal (Oriental and English together) was 291, and the expenditure on this account was nearly Rs.50,000. In 1844 another step had been taken which gave ultimately a far stronger impetus to English education. On the 10th of October in that year appeared Lord Hardinge's resolution definitely enjoining the selection for Government service of candidates who had received an English education. It was directed against lingering prejudices, though it must not be supposed that young men who had learnt English in the new colleges were altogether shut out from service under Government. On the contrary, success in obtaining employment had been from the first one of the incentives to English education; but Lord Hardinge's Educational resolution lays down definitely selection on educational grounds as a principle. The exact words of the resolution are of interest: "The Governor-General having taken into consideration the existing state of education in Bengal, and being of opinion that it is highly desirable to afford it every reasonable encouragement by holding out to those who have taken advantage of the opportunities afforded them a fair prospect of employment in the Public Service and thereby not only to reward individual merit, but to enable the State to profit as largely and as early as possible, by the result of the measures adopted of late years for the instruction of the people, as well by the Government as by private individuals and Societies, has resolved that in every possible case a preference shall be given in the selection of candidates for public employment to those who have been educated in the institutions thus established and especially to those who have distinguished themselves therein by a more than ordinary degree of merit and attainment." The immediate effect of this resolution does not appear to have been great: its ultimate influence has been scarcely less than that of the adoption of English education. For it has given English education its value in terms of livelihood. A third measure has been equally, or even more, influential in determining the supremacy attained by English education. This is the adoption of English as the language of public business. This had been contemplated as the settled policy of Government as early as 1829, when, in reply to the Committee of Public Instruction, a Government letter says that "his Lordship in Council has no hesitation in stating to your Committee, and in authorizing you to announce to all concerned in the superintendence of your native seminaries that it is the wish and admitted policy of the British Government to render its own language gradually and eventually the language of public business throughout the country; and that it will omit no opportunity of giving every reasonable and practicable degree of encouragement to the execution of this project." This was in the first year of Lord William Bentinck's administration. Here again it is not the immediate but the ultimate effects of the policy which were important. When Persian was first abolished in the Courts, its place was taken by the vernaculars, and in 1838 Charles Trevelyan was able to write: "Everybody is now agreed in giving the preference to the vernacular language."[1] The claim of the vernacular has never since been lost sight of, yet broadly English now is and has long been the language of public business. It is to be observed indeed that this measure and also the employment in the work of public administration of the men of the new learning were only logical consequences of the decision of Government to promote English education actively. Their importance in contributing to the ultimate result, the rapid spread of English education, must not on that account be overlooked in a just appreciation of cause and effect. English education has not extended solely by its own intrinsic value. Three factors have cooperated: (1) educational organization determined by the decision of 1835; (2) the policy of requiring more and more a knowledge of English as a condition of

[1] Trevelyan, "On the Education of the People of India," p. 148.

employment in the public services in all but the lowest positions; (3) the more and more complete adoption of English as the language of public business. These causes, moreover, are interlaced, and act and react each upon the others.

The course of events in other parts of India was roughly similar. In Bombay there were in 1834 two schools under English masters; 214 students of English in one and 100 in the other. In 1835 the total number under instruction (Vernacular and English) was 5018. In 1840 the first report of the Board of Education gives a total of 7426 and for the Elphinstone Institution 681. In 1850–51 the total in Government schools and colleges is 13,460 and for English education 2066.

The advance in Madras was less rapid. As we have seen, it was not till 1837 that Madras had a school teaching English at all, and not till 1841 that a Government institution resembling the Hindu College, Calcutta, was opened. This was called the Madras "University," and consisted of two departments, a High School and a College. Numbers in this place of education did not ever reach 200 up to the year 1852. On the other hand, the work of Missionary Societies in Madras was comparatively extensive. By the year 1852 the total number of Mission Schools in the Madras Presidency was 1185 and of pupils 38,005. Also the Madras Christian College had between 200 and 300 pupils, while still known as the General Assembly's School.

Returns laid before the House of Lords in 1852 give the totals in the three Presidencies and the North West Provinces of Bengal: 25,372 under instruction, 9893 for English education, and an expenditure of Rs.7,14,597. These figures obviously exclude all but Government institutions. Then came the epoch-making despatch of

1854. From 1835 to 1854, it may be noted in passing, is nineteen years, a time equal to the interval between 1910 and 1891. The despatch itself is by far the most impressive measure of the advance made.

The despatch of 1854 is important on every account in the history of Indian education, and is quite rightly looked upon as a charter of educational privilege. It was the first authoritative declaration of policy on the part of the sovereign power responsible for the administration of British India—at that time still the Court of Directors. The policy therein defined is that which to-day controls the system in operation throughout the Indian Empire, and is co-extensive in scope with the whole field of education. It ordained the formation of Departments of Public Instruction. It promised the establishment of Universities and sketched the university scheme in full detail. All the lines of Public Instruction as we know them now in successive departmental reports and university calendars are laid in this comprehensive document. There is even one thing more which it is acknowledged has been imperfectly attended to and which is destined, perhaps, to mark the next great era of advance, a plain recognition of the importance of measures to convey "useful and practical knowledge" to the great mass of the people.

The occasion of the despatch was the renewal of the Company's charter by Parliament in 1853. Lord Dalhousie was then Viceroy, and the great material reforms which he initiated were then in progress. Education was engaging his anxious attention when the despatch of Sir Charles Wood[1] came bringing "a scheme of education for all India, far wider and more comprehensive than the Local or the Supreme Government would have

[1] Raised to the peerage in 1866 as Viscount Halifax.

ventured to suggest." It will be convenient to give separate treatment to each of the main parts of the scheme indicated above, examining the details, investigating how far they have been carried out in the established system, and reviewing the results actually achieved. It will be convenient also to vary the order so far as to take first the universities, because they are more directly in the line of advance from the resolution of 1835. But first the preliminary statement of policy may be briefly considered. "Among many subjects of importance," says the despatch, "none have a stronger claim to our attention than that of education. It is one of our most sacred duties to be the means, as far as in us lies, of conferring upon the natives of India those vast moral and material blessings which flow from the general diffusion of useful knowledge, and which India may under Providence derive from her connection with England." A little further on it declares emphatically "that the education which we desire to see extended in India is that which has for its object the diffusion of the improved arts, science, philosophy, and literature of Europe; in short, of European knowledge." The despatch pays a fitting tribute to the antiquarian and historical interest of the classical languages of India and to the honourable and influential position of those who maintain the traditional learning. It explicitly repudiates any aim or desire "to substitute the English language for the vernacular dialects of the country." In these respects it makes good the temperamental defects of Macaulay's minute. At the same time it says as plainly as Macaulay that "the systems of science and philosophy which form the learning of the East abound with grave errors, and Eastern literature is at best very deficient as regards all modern discovery and improvements; Asiatic learning, therefore, however widely diffused, would but little advance our object." It affirms that "a knowledge of English will always be essential to those natives of India who aspire to a high order of education." It expresses the desire "of extending far more widely the means of acquiring general European knowledge of a less high order, but of such a character as may be practically useful to the people of India in their different spheres of life." It regrets a tendency which it fears has been created "to neglect the study of the vernacular language." Consequently it lays down that "in any general system of education, the English language should be taught where there is a demand for it; but such instruction should always be combined with a careful attention to the study of the vernacular languages of the district, and with such general instruction as can be conveyed through that language." For the mass of the people, the authors of the despatch hold, the only possible medium of instruction is the mother-tongue; but it is significant that while this conviction is stated very plainly it is also indicated that the teachers themselves should know English. The general scope of the whole is "to decide on the mode in which the assistance of Government should be afforded to the more extended and systematic promotion of general education in India, and on the measures to be adopted to that end."

Unquestionably, the despatch of 1854 is a most memorable document. It rises to the height of its problem and comprehends its length and breadth. It outlines a complete and systematic organization of education in India from the university to the elementary school. In the fifty-six years that have passed since it was received, Government, the Education Departments, and private effort have toiled and panted at the tasks it set; they are straining at them still, and adequate fulfilment is not even yet within view. For it is nothing short of a complete system of national education which it sketches. The despatch of 1854 is thus the climax in the history of Indian education: what goes before leads up to it; what follows flows from it. It offers a convenient measure both of attainment and of failure of attainment. It will repay, therefore, the most careful study in relation to the problems of to-day.

VII

THE FOUNDATION AND GROWTH OF UNIVERSITIES

THE Indian universities owe their origin to the despatch of 1854. Already, nine years earlier, in 1845, a proposal for establishing a central university had been made by the Council of Education (the name by which the Committee of Public Instruction had been called since 1842), and put aside by the Court of Directors as premature. It is not difficult to understand the motives which influenced those who advocated the establishment of a university, or universities. The first successes of English education had been striking. In point of mere number we have seen the Hindu College reaching a total of 562 pupils in the year 1841. In 1851 there were 1464 students in the four Bengal colleges, the colleges at Hooghly, Dacca, and Krishnaghar, and the Hindu College, Calcutta, besides 227 studying English at the Sanskrit college, and two Madrasas (Calcutta and Hooghly): the total number sharing in English education was 4341. On the other hand, the standard attained by individuals was creditably high. In the early years the remarkable quickness and powers of expression of the students of the new learning were regarded with a sort of gaping wonder. The scholarship examination offered a strong incentive to effort, and afforded a more solid and definite test of attainment.

The answers "of the Most Proficient students in the Presidency and Mofussil Colleges" were year by year printed in the General Reports of Public Instruction, and very fairly bear out the claims made for the standard reached. When, after 1844, this examination was made a gate to the public service, there was already, as Sir Frederick Halliday said, "the germ of a university." It was natural that the need should be felt for some more distinctive recognition of academic attainment for the "large and annually increasing number of highly educated pupils." The Council, in 1845, calls it "a matter of strict justice and necessity." Naturally, a university was thought of, and degrees like those of European universities; and the London University, which had been established only in 1836, afforded a convenient model, for it was an examining and non-resident university. So, when the subject was brought up before Parliament in 1852, and evidence both for and against universities taken, the advocates of universities for India carried the day. At all events, the complete scheme of the Indian university as we know it is found in the Despatch of 1854, and in 1857 the universities were incorporated by Acts dated January 24th for Calcutta, for Bombay July 18th, and for Madras September 5th.

The first Entrance Examination of the Calcutta University was held in April, 1857. There were 244 candidates, and 162 passed. Within five years there were over a thousand candidates, and nearly five hundred passes. In the eleventh year (1867) there were 1507 candidates. In 1871 there were 1902. In 1881 there were 2937. In 1891 there were 5032. In 1901 there were 6135, and the number passed was 3307. This certainly looks, as far as figures can show it, like an effective demand for university education.

Or take it on the financial side. In 1857 the University cost Government Rs.11,918. In 1872-73, though its total expenditure had risen to Rs.46,519, it was just self-supporting. In 1873-74 there was a small but substantial balance of Rs.6236. In 1906, when for several years the expenditure had exceeded two-and-a-half lakhs, a reserve fund of over six lakhs had accumulated. As a practical business concern the University must also be pronounced a success. In these two respects, growth of numbers and financial independence, the University had certainly, by the end of the century, justified its promoters. These things were precisely what they had prophesied for it. "The adoption of the plan," the Council had said, "would only be attended with a very trifling expense to Government in the commencement; for, in the course of a few years, the proceeds of the Fee Fund would be more than sufficient to defray every expense attendant upon the University." At Convocation in 1866, nine years from the foundation of the University, Sir Henry Maine, in urging the necessity of university buildings, had said: "The thing must be seen to be believed. I do not know which was the more astonishing, more striking—the multitude of the students, who if not now, will soon, be counted not by the hundred, but by the thousand; or the keenness and eagerness which they displayed. For my part, I do not think anything of the kind has been seen by any European University since the Middle Ages, and I doubt whether there is anything founded by, or connected with, the British Government in India which excites so much practical interest in native households of the better class, from Calcutta to Lahore, as the examinations of this university."

If the question be asked, as it has been asked any

time these fifty years past, "Was the foundation of universities in India premature? Was the Calcutta University wisely and timely founded?" it would seem that at least a *primâ fácie* case for an affirmative answer lay patent in the bare facts of its practical success. And yet, somehow, the latter end has been confessedly unsatisfactory, and the last five years have been given to a continued effort at university reform. How came it that, in addressing Convocation in 1901, the Vice-Chancellor said: "It is not putting the case too strongly to say that, by many persons well qualified to judge, our whole university system is regarded with critical suspicion, or with positive disapproval?" Among the critics was an Indian editor, who wrote: "If education be the transmission of life from the living through the living to the living, we do not know how to describe the system of teaching that prevails here. It is carrying death from the dead through the dead to the dead." Something must have been wrong somewhere; something must have been overlooked; some latent defect must have been admitted into the system and allowed to grow, that, after forty years of flowing success and expansion, such statements should have been barely possible. What was it?—Possibly a more careful scrutiny may discover it.

First, it has to be observed that, though by 1901 the three original universities of Bombay, Calcutta, and Madras had all grown greatly, and two later universities had been added, the question of the ripeness of the times for the establishment of a university in 1857 is almost purely a question of Bengal. It was in Calcutta that the proposal for a university was put forward; it was in Bengal only that the conditions justifying the proposal subsisted. In 1857, when the order for the establishment of universities came, there was but one college in Madras with 302 students; in Bombay there were two colleges with 103 between them, whereas in the Lower Provinces of Bengal there were fourteen colleges, public and private, and the students in them numbered 921; without counting four colleges in the North-west Provinces and Oudh and their students. There is not less significant contrast in the development of the universities. In 1857, as already said, 162 candidates passed the Calcutta Entrance Examination; 54 passed the Madras Matriculation: no examination was held in Bombay. The first Bombay examination was not till 1859, and then 122 passed. In 1867 the number for Madras was 338; for Bombay 163; for Bengal 814. In the first fourteen years, from 1857 to 1870, the total number of students who had matriculated at the three Indian universities was 11,093, and of this total 7560, or rather over two-thirds belong to Bengal; only 1227 to Bombay. A comparison of figures for graduation gives similar results. There is a total of 856 graduates from 1858 to 1870, and of these 577, or again over two-thirds, belong to Calcutta. Of the 279 remaining, 163 graduated at Madras, 116 at Bombay. The question, then, of due preparedness for university organization and ambitions is primarily a question for Calcutta. In the Despatch itself the definite proposal of universities is made for Calcutta and Bombay only: the Council of Education in Calcutta and the Board of Education in Bombay were, with additional members, to constitute the Senates of the new universities. A university at Madras was made conditional on the existence of a sufficient number of institutions, from which properly qualified candidates could be supplied.

The contrast between the rapid extension of university

education in Bengal, and the slow advance in Bombay and Madras in these early years is very marked. Is it possible that in this contrast we may find a clue to the ultimate dissatisfaction with university progress? At a later epoch there was to be an equally rapid expansion in Madras, and in numbers the Madras University was sometimes to outstrip Calcutta; but that was not as yet. Mr. Arthur Howell, of the Bengal Civil Service, in reviewing "Education in British India" in 1871, notices two objections "not infrequently raised against the Calcutta University." One of these, that the University fails to encourage the Eastern classical languages in the manner intended by the Despatch of 1854, he meets easily by showing that Sanskrit and Arabic studies have not been neglected, and gain rather than lose by association with the new methods of education. The second is more serious; "that, looking to the poor and superficial acquirements of the great mass of those who obtain university distinctions, and to the fact that such distinctions are not pursued for their own sake, but merely as a means to employment or reward, there is really no *status* as yet for a university in the European sense of the term." This charge he excuses but does not altogether repel. He recognizes that "the pursuit of high culture for its own sake is rare in India, and certainly in Bengal," but continues: "Even admitting that the distinctions conferred by the Indian universities are poor and superficial, it may still be said that there is clearly a need of the kind of institution which Indian universities aspire to be, that is a practical and uniform test of the schools and colleges of high education, many of which are maintained by Government."

Surely the key to the mystery lies in the consideration of quality. The success of Calcutta University, the figures quoted above, and all those published year by year for all the universities, from 1871 right on to 1900, which afford such obvious material for congratulation, concern the quantitative extension of education only. They tell nothing of its intent or quality. What, it may be asked, was the real value of the education being given year by year to wider circles of young men? What precautions had been taken to secure that the men sent out with university degrees should be in a true sense educated? It is of special interest to notice what guidance the Despatch of 1854 affords on this point. It has something to say about the standard for degrees, though, naturally, what it says is expressed only in general terms. It suggests a twofold standard; a standard for "common degrees," and a standard for honours. As to the standard for honours, the Despatch is not in doubt: "care should be taken to maintain such a standard as will afford a guarantee for high ability and valuable attainments." The standard for the ordinary degree presents difficulty; it "will require to be fixed with very great judgment." The definition which the Despatch suggests is, that "the standard required should be such as to command respect, without discouraging the efforts of deserving students." This is by no means a precise definition, yet, perhaps, it serves well enough as a touchstone of attainment. It is manifest that the degrees of the Indian universities, more especially the Calcutta degree, did not, in 1901, "command respect." That they did not was one of the great impelling forces to reform.

VIII

THE COMMISSION OF 1882

CAREFUL enough attention has not been paid of recent years to the influence of the recommendations of the Education Commission of 1882 in determining the development of education in India between 1882 and 1900. In relation to the present undertaking they demand attention very specially, because one of the tendencies of the present time is in a direction precisely opposite to the most important and far-reaching of its recommendations; while others of its important recommendations, which have been allowed to fall out of view, are among those being now specially pressed for consideration.

The reasons given for the appointment of the Commission were the length of time that had elapsed since the Despatch of 1854 and the consequent expediency of "a more careful examination into the results attained and into the working of the present arrangements than has hitherto been attempted." It was really due largely to outside agitation and to the pledges given by the Marquis of Ripon before leaving England in 1880 for a thorough and searching inquiry how far the prescriptions of the despatch had been followed. The precise instructions given to the Commission were accordingly "to inquire particularly . . . into the manner in which effect has been given to the principles of the Despatch of

1854; and to suggest such measures as it may think desirable in order to the further carrying out of the policy therein laid down." There were "certain limitations" of the field of inquiry, and it is specially noteworthy that "the general working of the Indian Universities" was one of the subjects so excepted. The exception did not, however, extend to University education as carried on in the colleges.

The Commission was appointed in February, 1882. Sir William Hunter (at the time Member of the Viceroy's Legislative Council) was President: Mr. B. L. Rice, Director of Public Instruction, Mysore and Coorg, was Secretary; and there were twenty other members, including Sir Sayyid Ahmed, Mr. A. M. Bose, Sir Alfred Croft, Sir William Lee Warner, Dr. Miller of Madras, Babu Bhudeb Mookerjee and Maharaja Sir Jotendro Mohan Tagore. The Commission first deliberated for some seven weeks in Calcutta. Then for eight months evidence was collected locally in the various provinces, and the President made a tour in order to hold sessions and examine witnesses. "A great enthusiasm," writes Mr. Satthianadhan, "was excited on the subject of education throughout the length and breadth of the country. At every place that was visited large meetings were held to welcome the Commission." Nearly two hundred witnesses were examined and over three hundred memorials were presented. Further deliberations followed in Calcutta from December, 1882, to March, 1883. Two hundred and twenty-two resolutions were passed, one hundred and eighty unanimously. The report, which was drawn up by a committee of six, extends to over six hundred folio pages.

The most far-reaching of the recommendations were those which concerned the withdrawal of Government from higher education. Something of this had been tentatively put forward in the Government Resolution appointing the Commission, as a subject for consideration. The Despatch of 1854 had introduced "grants-in-aid" because of "the impossibility of Government alone doing all that must be done" for the organization of education in India. Grants-in-aid were intended to encourage self-help and foster "a spirit of reliance upon local exertions." Local management under Government inspection, stimulated by grants-in-aid, was to supplement and finally, perhaps, in large measure, to supersede direct management by Government. The aim of the Commission was to carry the transfer of direct management further. Their recommendations are carefully guarded, but the net result is the affirmation of gradual withdrawal as definitely the aim of Government policy. This is implied or hinted in various places; the explicit recommendation is "that all Directors of Public Instruction aim at the gradual transfer to local native management of Government schools of secondary instruction (including schools attached to first or second grade colleges) in every case in which the transfer can be effected without lowering the standard, or diminishing the supply of education, and without endangering the permanence of the institution transferred." This explicit recommendation concerned only secondary schools, and it seemed to be carefully safeguarded by qualifying conditions. The practical result in the long run was the partial withdrawal of Government from the direct conduct of higher education; and conversely the imparting of a strong stimulus to the founding of schools and colleges by private enterprise. This was in fact the result deliberately and expressly aimed at. "We venture to hope," says the report in concluding on this subject,

" that the line of action we have marked out in the above recommendations will result, not all at once, yet with no longer interval than is always required for changes fruitful of large results, in public sentiment taking a direction which will lead to the gradual and, by and by, to the rapid transfer to bodies of native gentlemen of the institutions now maintained by Government." It all reads very plausibly in the pages of the report, and a great deal is said of the need of caution that the highest educational interests should not suffer, and of due care for the maintenance of high standards. The question is, was it really wise to put forward at that time such recommendations at all, and were the salutary precautions enjoined successfully taken?

There were many minor recommendations, all having as their object " to improve and strengthen the position of aided schools " as the complement to the policy of Government withdrawal. One of them runs, " That in order to encourage the establishment of aided schools, the managers be not required to charge fees as high as those of a neighbouring Government school of the same class." This is for schools: there is a similar recommendation for colleges:—" That while it is desirable to affirm the principle that fees at the highest rate consistent with the undiminished spread of education should be levied in every college aided by the State, no aided college should be required to levy fees at the same rate as that charged in a neighbouring Government college." On the surface perhaps these recommendations read very innocently. If they are attentively considered, it will be found that their natural effect must be to undermine the very possibility of sound education. The more carefully they are examined, the more plainly will it appear that they are largely, if not mainly, responsible for the state of University education which the reform movement of 1901 to 1906 set out to remedy. For could anything have been better calculated to promote the spread of inefficiency, to bring about what has actually resulted—the multiplication of schools and colleges insufficiently staffed, miserably equipped, utterly unfit to give useful education? The more directly injurious provision was the authorization of low fees, which effectually secured that new schools and colleges founded by private enterprise should be of a weak and inefficient type. It is true that another rule proposed ran, "that the Director of Public Instruction should, in consultation with the managers of schools receiving aid from Government, determine the scale of fees to be charged and the proportion of pupils to be exempted from payment therein." There was, however, opposition to the carrying out of this proviso, and even in Madras, where it had been the practice for many years before the Commission, it was ultimately dropped. The second Quinquennial Review of the Progress of Education in India, written by Mr. Nash and published in 1893, makes this significant comment: "The reason for this change of system is not given in the reports, but probably it was due to the difficulty experienced by aided schools in competing with unaided schools in which lower fees could be charged; in some cases the managers of aided schools resigned the grants in order to be able to reduce the fees." It would be difficult within reasonable compass to bring out the full tale of evils—ill-paid and incompetent teachers, overcrowded class-rooms, bad buildings, poor school furniture—with which that one sentence is pregnant. The calamitous significance of what was happening is only grasped when it is considered that for many schools which came into existence under these influences the fees were almost the sole source of income. Common sense would have dictated a rule the very reverse of that enunciated by the Commission; that the private schools and colleges should be empowered to charge higher fees, not lower. The Government schools and colleges had other resources, and did not depend on the fee fund for their proper up-keep. The private schools and colleges, on the other hand, were for the most part unendowed and, except in the case of missionary institutions, had seldom any revenues other than those derived from fees. Fees were to them all-important; for they drew their whole support from them. To give, as it were, authoritative countenance to low fees was to ensure the inevitable and lasting inefficiency of the institutions. It remains only further for the careful historian to remark that some of the schools and colleges equipped and staffed on this promising basis have actually at times worked to private profit.

In another important division of education the express prescription of the Commission of 1882 has been discredited by experience. The Commission adopted for elementary schools the system of payment by results which at that time still ruled in Great Britain. Their recommendation is "That preference be given to that system which regulates the aid given mainly according to the results of examinations." "This system," writes Mr. Orange in the last Quinquennial Review of Indian Education, "notorious by the name, of payment by results is universally acknowledged to have been a failure wherever it has been introduced." The Commission of 1882 was not, then, infallible, and it is open to us to disagree with its findings, if we see reason to do so. Many of them were undoubtedly sound and judicious and have been absorbed into the educational system. Such were the rules and regulations limiting the removal of pupils from one school to another, now known as "Transfer Rules;" their recommendations about Text Book Committees, Normal Schools, Educational Conferences, Departmental Codes of Rules, and many other matters of educational interest, great and small. In some matters recommendations, in themselves excellent, have proved in advance of the times, in so far as they have remained up to the present a dead letter. Such are the suggestions of the formation of "a general educational library and museum at some suitable locality in each Province," and that "in the upper classes of high schools there be two divisions—one leading to the Entrance examination of the Universities, the other of a more practical character, intended to fit youths for commercial and other non-literary pursuits." As regards the latter, heroic attempts have indeed been made to divert a branch stream from the main current of high school education, but up to the time of the last Quinquennial Review, "ninety-five per cent. of the boys who pass through secondary schools follow the curricula prescribed by the Universities for the Matriculation examination." The important recommendation that "as a general rule transfers of officers from Professorships of colleges to Inspectorships of schools, and *vice versâ*, be not made," has been partially adopted through sheer force of circumstances, but has yet to receive the recognition its importance as a fundamental principle requires. Very great stress was laid by the Commission on the moral side of education. In relation to every stage of education they call marked attention to its importance. Of Primary schools they say, "That all inspecting officers and teachers be directed to see that all the teaching and discipline of every school are such as to exert a right influence on the manner and conduct and the character of the children. . . ." Similarly, of Secondary schools, "That the importance of requiring inspecting officers to see that the teaching and discipline of every school are such as to exert a right influence on the manners, the conduct and the character of pupils, be re-affirmed." For colleges they recommend "Lectures on the duties of a man and a citizen," and a "moral text-book." The latter is still a debated but, on the whole, discredited proposal. The supreme importance of the education of character is taking a prominent place among the questions of the hour.

In the details of school management and of educational organization the Commission of 1882 is generally right. It is on the larger question of policy that its conclusions are disputable. The largest of all has only so far been noticed by implication, and this, the place of Primary education in the educational scheme for India, is also the question which is again at the present time being specially pressed for attention. The views of the Commission are clear and uncompromising. It is Elementary education, indigenous or departmental, which has the first claim. The claims of higher education to State aid are only legitimate when the requirements of popular education have been adequately met. They recommend specifically "That primary education be declared to be that part of the whole system of Public Instruction which possesses an almost exclusive claim on local funds set apart for education and a large claim on provincial revenues." Again: "That while every branch of education can justly claim the fostering care of the State, it is desirable, in the present circumstances of the country, to declare the elementary education of the masses, its provision, extension and improvement, to be that part of the educational system to which the strenuous efforts of the

State should now be directed in a still larger measure than heretofore." So conversely of secondary education, "That it be distinctly laid down that the relation of the State to secondary is different from its relation to primary education in that the means of primary education may be provided without regard to the existence of local co-operation, while it is ordinarily expedient to provide the means of secondary education only where adequate local co-operation is forthcoming, and that, therefore, in all ordinary cases, secondary schools for instruction in English be hereafter established by the State preferably on the footing of the system of Grants-in-aid." There is plausibility in this statement of principle, and it has all the weight that the analogy of European countries can give it. Is it, however, the right principle for India, and is it practically applicable at the present time? These are momentous questions, and a good deal of ground has still to be traversed in these papers before we are in a position to answer them with a clear perception of the issues. We require first to study the character and causes of university reform; and then to make some independent survey of secondary and primary school education in India as each of these has been developed under the influence of the Despatch of 1854 and the Commission of 1882.

IX

UNIVERSITY REFORM 1901–1906

THE causal connection suggested in the course of the review of the recommendations of the Commission of 1882 is this. The affirmation by Government of a policy of "gradual withdrawal" from higher education coupled with a virtual approbation of low fees led to a rapid expansion of university education between 1882 and 1890; but this rapid expansion involved a disastrous sacrifice of the essential conditions of sound education. Statistics are notoriously fallacious, and figures, it is known, obey the powerful spells of those who charm with them; but here the figures as they stand recorded in university tables and in successive reviews of educational progress are so plain and straightforward that mistake of their meaning is hardly conceivable. There are complicating circumstances, it is true, if one analyses the figures searchingly, but broadly there was extraordinary expansion in the years immediately following 1882. For schools the most striking comparisons are those of the first five years. For 1881–2 the total of pupils in secondary English schools is given in the first general review of education in India as 149,233. For 1884–5 the total is 254,802, an increase of over 100,000 in three years; for 1886–7 it is 271,654, an increase of 120,000 in five years. By 1891–2 the figures of 1881–2 are just doubled, standing at slightly over three hundred thousand. Numbers have advanced steadily since, but never at a rate so rapid. At the end of the next ten years the total is 422,187; and the latest tables available, those for 1906–7, give 473,130. These figures are not, however, exactly apposite to the present inquiry, since owing to a principle of classification adopted in 1883, Middle English Schools are included along with High Schools in the totals recorded. Our direct concern is now with High Schools only. The estimate of the Commission of 1882 for pupils in High Schools at that date is 65,448, and the total for 1901 is given in the last general review as 251,626, but for the intervening years the figures are not recorded. The statistics of matriculation afford a more accurate measure for present purposes. For Bengal the Entrance Examination certainly indicates roughly the advance of High School as well as of collegiate education. All the higher secondary schools that came into being were of one type. All aspired to send up candidates to the Entrance Examination. Many had (and have except for a compulsory limit now) congested Entrance classes. Again there is a roughly (very roughly) constant proportion between the number of candidates at the Entrance Examination and the number actually matriculated; and again a roughly constant variation between the number of matriculates and the number of candidates at the degree examinations. Thus the matriculation examination affords a fairly accurate measure, at all events in Bengal, of the extension of higher education. Adopting this as a rough measure generally, we see that in 1882 the total of candidates for matriculation in the three universities then existing was 7429. In 1885–6 the total for India is 13,093, nearly double in four years, and in 1889 it is 19,138. The further increase to 1906 is under six thousand, making a total of 24,963. Looking separately to Bengal—and it is with Bengal that university reform is connected in its causes and inception as well as the beginning of universities—we find that in 1872 the number of candidates at the Entrance Examination had been just over 2000 (2144). In 1882 it was just over 3000. In 1885 it was 4317. In 1888 it was 6134, more than doubling the 3000 of 1882. The total only once exceeded this maximum between 1888 and 1900, namely, in the year 1900 itself with 6309; but it never fell below 5000. From 1902 on the number was always over 7000, till in 1907 it fell to 5290.

Now, if the Matriculation Examination of Calcutta University had been a satisfactory test as a school leaving examination, and if the education of the colleges had been sound and good, this wonderful expansion between 1882 and 1888—these are the most significant dates—could only have been cause for rejoicing. Naturally it seemed such to those who lived through those exhilarating years, and who did not scrupulously assay the value of the results attained. Address after address at Convocation vibrates with subdued elation, though now and again, it is true, the attentive listener catches an undertone of misgiving. Any one who wishes to enter vividly into the feelings of that time, and to obtain a graphic view of the forces at work in the Calcutta university, of what was admirable in it as well as what was of hurtful tendency, cannot do better than read Sir Courtney Ilbert's widely ranging and exceedingly instructive address of December 19th, 1885. An important series of changes in the arrangements for the Arts Examination had just been brought to completion. Numbers still showed a marked and rapid increase. The dominant tone is one of satisfaction and congratulation. Of the revised courses, he says: "As far as I can judge, they appear to me to be entirely in the right direction. . . . Their tendency is towards greater specialization and concentration at the later stages of the university course, and thus towards more exact and thorough knowledge of the subjects which the student applies himself to master." He is able to say of the honours men of the university that "not only is the number of graduates in Honours steadily increasing, but the highest standard which they attain is steadily rising." There is only one sentence in the speech which suggests another side to the picture, but that sentence is significant. "As collegiate education has become more common," says the speaker, "the value of the symbol which denotes it has proportionately fallen." It is not, however, till 1889 that we definitely hear of over-production as a criticism to be met, when Lord Lansdowne, as Chancellor, said: "I am afraid that we must not disguise from ourselves that if our schools and colleges continue to educate the youth of India at the present rate, we are likely to hear even more than we do at present of the complaint that we are turning out every year an increasing number of young men whom we have provided with an intellectual equipment, admirable in itself, but practically useless to them, on account of the small number of openings which the professions afford for gentlemen who have received this kind of education." But in Convocation addresses the voice of criticism is in these years almost wholly silent. We must look elsewhere for strict scrutiny of the intrinsic value of what was outwardly such a triumphant progress. Nor do we look for it vainly. For there were always some among educational workers who looked more carefully into the education which was being so rapidly extended and raised their voices against uncritical satisfaction. As early even as 1860 two leading educationalists in the North-West Provinces, Mr. Reid, Director of Public Instruction, and Mr. Kempson, Principal of the Bareilly College, warned the university of the dangers of a too ambitious course of studies and of education lacking accuracy and depth. It is not, however, from direct and express criticism that we get the illuminating flashes which enable in retrospect the sharpened vision of the inquirer to discern how the way was surely prepared for a catastrophe of some kind, but in things incidentally written in relation to some question of the hour without any directly critical intention. For instance, in 1871, the head of a Calcutta college, writing *apropos* of certain wide proposals from the North-West Provinces, said: "From what I know of University students I should hardly regard the knowledge of English possessed by those who pass in the *second* class at the First Arts Examination as sufficient; and certainly I should hold the knowledge of a student who passed in the third class to be insufficient." In 1870, out of 520 candidates for this examination 28 passed in the first division, 108 in the second, and 97 in the third. In the same series of opinions another correspondent laments that under the existing system a class of men who might be called "mere machines of memory" was multiplying very fast. "Education," he says, "has too long been viewed in Bengal as the cramming in a large amount of ill-digested knowledge—memory has been cultivated to the exclusion of the higher faculties; and a class of students has been produced who, whatever crammed book-knowledge they possess, have, with a few noble exceptions, neither original ideas nor the power of observing or judging for themselves." This, be it carefully noted, was before the great expansion between 1882 and 1888, and, be it further observed, that between 1871 and 1900 nothing whatever was done to improve the standard of English which was absolutely vital to a system of education deliberately and avowedly carried on in English.

The extreme importance of the sufficiency of the standard of English at the Entrance Examination does not, indeed, seem to have been adequately realized either in the early years of the university or in the years of growing prosperity following on the Commission of 1882. In 1886 and 1887 a Committee was engaged in considering the Calcutta Entrance Examination. Opinions were sought on all sides, from heads of colleges and others. It is a remarkable fact that though the questions of standard were warmly canvassed, scarcely a single voice was raised on behalf of an adequate standard in English. Most of the opinions are mere verbiage. One letter there is, however, which is remarkable as going to the root of the matter, and laying bare one of the causes which ultimately made some reform of the system necessary. "I am sorry," says the writer, "to find that beyond the proposal . . . not a single modification has been introduced tending to remedy the so universally recognized evil, viz. that the University examinations, and perhaps more particularly the Entrance Examination, favour memory work more than is desirable, and that cram is sufficient to secure a pass. Any one acquainted with the practical work of preparing Indian students for these examinations must confess in all fairness that degrees are at a low ebb." A curious commentary this, on the Vice-Chancellor's address at the end of 1885, but it is the commentary of the teacher actually engaged upon the work and knowing it. He adds a little later: "Without anything like a complete course of general education, any candidate gifted with a good memory is sure to carry off his Entrance certificate. And this is mainly to be ascribed to the appointment of text-books in every subject, containing all that a student is expected to answer at the examination."

Perhaps, however, the most significant clue is that unconsciously afforded by a naïve sentence in the Convocation address of 1883. Speaking of the success of the first two lady graduates, the Vice-Chancellor said that they had really done better than their places in the list showed. "I heard," he says, "from one of the examiners, that though their answers in his subject were not framed so as to secure the highest number of marks, the papers showed an originality, a thoroughness, and a real comprehension of the subject, which gave him a high opinion of the intellectual power of the writers." Examinations which did not secure the highest marks to intellectual power, to originality, thoroughness, and a real comprehension of the subject! A horde of candidates securing passes by memorizing text-books out of a ludicrously deficient knowledge of English! In these things surely there was a good deal for which a remedy had to be found.

How vital the question of the standard of English at the gates of the university really is, is at once manifest on steadily facing the fact that all the studies of the university were and are to be carried on through English. A student who does not start with a competent knowledge of English has obviously no chance of getting on even terms with his studies. He is heavily handicapped from the beginning, and, unless he goes to school again and learns English, the handicap is never likely to be taken off, even if by good or bad luck he ultimately obtains a degree. In this vital matter nothing was done to raise the standard; some things were done to lower the standard; and always there was a steady pressure from the weaker schools and colleges, from year to year increasing in number under the influence of the plausible doctrines of the Commission of 1882, tending to lower standards. Is it wonderful that between 1890 and 1900, dissatisfaction grew everywhere, though it did not very often voice itself in public; or that in 1894, a writer in the *Calcutta Review*, who found the remedy in a gradual raising of the standard in the Entrance Examination, and the maintenance by Government of schools of a higher type, said openly: "We are spreading English education through the length and breadth of these lands on a system which it is scarcely too harsh to call rotten"? When university reform came in strong flood in the year 1901, it did not come too soon.

It is too soon yet to judge in just perspective the reform movement of the years which follow between 1901 and 1906. It is of profound interest to all concerned with university work in India, and when its history comes to be fully written, that interest will not be diminished. The central fact is that it was (like the inception of English education) a movement from within, not from without; and that Englishmen and Indians co-operated in the task. The reform movement is associated with Lord Curzon's administration and with Lord Curzon's name, and as he bore unmerited obloquy on account of it, to him also must be assigned a large share of the praise, if ever praise is awarded. But for Lord Curzon's known interest in education and his force of character, it would not have come at that time; but that it came at all is most of all due to the persistence from 1860 onwards here and there of a few educational workers, who had more care for the reality of education than for the shows, and who had the true interests of students and universities at heart. Earlier attempts at initiating a reform movement there had been about the year 1895, but they never got beyond the stage of draft proposals. The sequence of events in the actual inception of reform was this. On February the 16th, 1901, after Lord Curzon had referred in carefully-guarded language to his intentions in regard to the university, the Vice-Chancellor said: "For the first time, the Chancellor asks the university to consider the possibility of constitutional reform." In March, a strong representation of the need for inquiry and action was made by a number of professors and heads of colleges. In September, a Conference was held at Simla which made a preliminary survey of the whole educational field. In January, 1902, the Indian Universities Commission was appointed. Their inquiries continued through February, March, and April. Their report was published in June.

University reform was initiated, as we have seen, in Bengal, and was directed by its initiators to the circumstances of Calcutta University. It was a debatable point whether the other universities needed reform for analogous reasons. The Commission came to the conclusion that they did, and recommended reform on similar lines in respect of constitution, examinations, courses of study, standards, social life. Two of the most salient recommendations were (1) that the Syndicate of each University should fix a minimum fee rate; (2) that so-called second-grade colleges should in process of time be eliminated. The publication of the report called forth an outburst of criticism. These two provisions, though educationally very weighty reasons can be given for their expediency, were assailed with special vehemence. Government gave way to the popular outcry on these two points, and announced their omission from the scheme of reform.

On these bases an Act to amend the law relating to the Universities of British India was introduced in 1904, and warmly debated in the Legislative Council. It received the assent of the Governor-General on the 24th of March, and took effect on the 1st of September, 1904. Then began a new phase of university history. New Senates and Syndicates came into office, appointed on the principle "that educational standards should be allowed a predominant influence" in the administration of a university; and set about the framing of a revised body of regulations. These, as finally approved by the Government of India for the University of Calcutta, came into operation in July 1906.

It is too early, as I have said, to judge confidently of the efficacy of the new constitutions and the new regulations. Lord Curzon claimed for his reforms—which in his view and intention embraced a much wider range than university education—that "out of them has been born a new life for higher education in India." This is certainly true. A definite impetus has been given to the improvement of both colleges and high schools under pressure of the new regulations; more money, much more money, is being spent on them. There is improvement in buildings, in staff, in equipment. There has been a real quickening of energies in all directions. The most conspicuous improvements in Bengal colleges have been two: (1) There has been a most marked improvement in the equipment and methods of science teaching. This is the greatest change of all, and amounts to no less than a revolution, a revolution pregnant with potentialities for the material progress of the country. (2) There has been a liberal strengthening of staffs. Government has voluntarily set the example in its own colleges; but everywhere pressure has been exerted by the Syndicate to induce colleges to raise their staffs in accordance with more exacting views of the requirements of efficient teaching. Unless the conditions laid down are conformed with, affiliation is refused; and this applies equally when the college asking affiliation is a Government college. The Syndicate has thus effective control. These are very important successes; and there are several more points on which there is assured ground for congratulation.

If we review this whole history of the reform movement fairly, we are bound to admit that the effort for reform was, in Bengal at all events, thoroughly justified; that Government policy has been sound in regard to it, erring, if anywhere, on the side of caution. We have good reason to hope that the education being given in the colleges this year is in important respects better than the education which was being given in 1905. Lord Curzon was justified in contending that this was a deliverance, a deliverance of true education from impediments and encumbrances. "It is," he said at Simla in 1905, shortly before leaving India, "the setting free of the service of education, by placing in authoritative control over education the best intellects and agencies that can be enlisted in the task, and it is the casting away of the miserable gyves and manacles that had been fastened on the limbs of the youths of India, stunting their growth, crippling their faculties, and tying them down." Such certainly is the aim, whether it is yet quite attained or not; and therefore Lord Curzon was justified in adding: "In my view we are entitled to the hearty co-operation of all patriotic Indians in the task, for it is their people we are working for, and their future we are trying to safeguard and enlarge."

X

HIGH ENGLISH SCHOOLS

REAL and substantial as have been the improvements effected already by university reform, there are one or two measures of importance which have quite definitely not been attempted, or not effected sufficiently. One is such a raising of fees as would at once hinder overcrowding in colleges and place the unendowed colleges on a better economic basis. Another, and that the most vital of all, is the raising of the standard of English at matriculation to the level of efficiency required by the nature of university studies. An improvement of standard, it may be hoped, has really been effected: there is reason to fear it is not yet adequate to the end in view, though the attainment of this end is an indispensable condition of sound work. Now the learning of English is the proper task not of the colleges, but of the schools. What of the high English schools and the education they are giving? Sound university education is unattainable without the improvement of high school education. That has been frankly recognized in the measures of reform already carried out. All the universities now definitely assume responsibility for the character of the schools allowed to send up candidates for matriculation. There are by the regulations "conditions of recognition" and the conditions are to be made real by effective inspection. All high schools alike are brought under this new control,

Government and non-Government, aided and unaided. A great deal of attention has been given to the subject of high English schools since the new regulations came into force. The Third Chapter in the last quinquennial review of educational progress is most illuminating on the whole subject. "There is," says Mr. Orange, "every indication that universities and departments are carrying out in earnest the powers and duties entrusted to them in respect of secondary schools seeking the privilege of University recognition." That was three years ago and the work has gone on steadily since. Conditions, as might be expected, vary greatly in the different provinces of India, but the conclusion of any general review of the schools in relation to the universities must be that the whole subject of high school education still demands unslackening attention. The two most general defects appear to be (1) poorly qualified teachers, (2) bad teaching of English; two points of vital import for collegiate education. Of the masters in high schools Mr. Orange writes: "Speaking generally, it may be said that the qualifications and the pay of teachers in secondary schools are below any standard that could be thought reasonable; and that the inquiries which are now being made into the subject have revealed a state of things that is scandalous in Bengal and Eastern Bengal, and is unsatisfactory in every province." As to teaching, while method in most subjects leaves much to be desired, in more than one province English is singled out as the subject worst taught. High school education is best in Bombay; taken in the lump it is worst in the sphere of Calcutta University. Good schools there are in Bengal and Eastern Bengal as well as in all other parts of India: it is the great number of weak and ill-equipped schools in certain provinces which makes the problem of raising all to a satisfactory standard of efficiency so difficult. But whatever the defects in teaching, discipline, buildings, equipment in Bengal and Eastern Bengal, or anywhere in India, the feature most deserving of notice at the present time is improvement. A genuine impetus towards improvement is visible everywhere, due to the heightened interest in education that has been general since 1901, and in a more special sense to the impulse of university reform. The signs are hopeful, provided the impetus is not allowed to die down, but is reinforced by further efforts, public and private.

Looking back to find the causes of the present unsatisfactory state of secondary education, there can be little doubt that the close subordination of high school education to a University Entrance examination, however natural and convenient it may have been in the beginning and is even now, has in the long run proved injurious to the best interests of education. It has in the first place established a false standard for schools and a wrong aim. School education should educate for life and should be circumscribed by no narrower aim. It should give an education relatively complete in itself. The further education of the university is necessarily for a limited number, not for all. To contract the education of all to the pattern of a preparatory course for university studies, and especially of university studies so peculiarly conditioned as they are in India, was to cripple school education. Next it has tended to limit schools to one type, whereas other types of schools have been wanted. In particular there has been need of better secondary schools with aims less scholastically ambitious and more practical than those of the high school working up to a university standard. A factor which has swayed disastrously here is the overweening ambition which has been so common an influence in the history of educational institutions in Bengal, each aiming at climbing out of its own class into the class next above it. Schools have seldom been content to moderate their ambitions by their resources, to rest satisfied in doing quiet work in a well-defined but limited sphere. The middle vernacular school aspires to be middle English; the middle English school to be a high school. High schools have schemed to be raised into second grade colleges, and the second grade college with better reason aspires to be first grade. This ambition, which in itself is sufficiently laudable, has, when unaccompanied by any proper sense of scale in education, proved harmful, by inciting the promoters of these institutions to press for the supposed higher status without any due regard to the standard of equipment and provision which the higher status requires. The resulting tendency has been to lower standards and produce general weakness. The saving truth that a good middle school is better than a bad high school and a good school immeasurably better than a weak and poorly equipped college has been wholly lost sight of. It has never been sufficiently realized how fundamental is the question of expense. The provision of schools of a higher standard entails expense according to an irreducible scale, the incidence of which can by no jugglery be avoided. If you want that kind of education, you *must* incur the expense. You can only cheapen the expense by lowering the quality, and then you do not get the education you want at all but a spurious imitation. This is a simple principle, absolutely fundamental, absolutely impossible of evasion. The refusal to admit these simple truths is the cause of the unsatisfactory nature of so much of the education given.

Every grade of school has its proper work to do, and

in doing it fills a useful place in the system as a whole. Well-organized high schools, the immediate subject here, are of special importance, in relation to the highest form of education, because the success of college education is based necessarily on the quality of high school education. Unless the education of the high schools is sound, college education cannot be sound. The neglect of this vital perception is what even now hampers the improvement of college education. Something has been done as was shown at the beginning of this paper. Much more remains to be done and can only be neglected at the risk of losing again the ground that has been gained by university reform. There is need of a fresh intuition, the intuition that the school is not less important than the college, but even more important. Indeed the mistake of the past in its ultimate expression is that the cardinal and incomparable value of school education has not been sufficiently realized. There can be no doubt now that serious harm has been done by the systematic subordination of the school to the college. The college has been magnified; the school has been depressed. But it is not true that a college is higher educationally than a school. On the contrary there are valid reasons why the school as an institution for education is more important than the college. In Great Britain the school has an easy primacy, and the special pride of England is her Public Schools rather than her Universities. The gift seemingly most easily within her power to give, a noble school education, England has not yet given to India. It is a pity it should be so. The names of English schools are world-famous. Who even in India has heard the name of any great Indian school! If names great in the field of education are thought of in England, it is the names of great schoolmasters that are thought of first—Colet, Mulcaster, Busby, Arnold, Thring, Ridding, Almond. Why are there no similar names in India? Why would it seem strange to speak even of "a great schoolmaster?" And yet, when Sir Alexander Arbuthnot, who later was twice Vice-Chancellor of Calcutta University, was addressing Convocation in Madras in 1868, he singled out as the man to be named first for greatness of character in the nineteenth century, not any statesman or soldier or man of letters, but Dr. Thomas Arnold of Rugby. We need in India to think more worthily of schools and schoolmasters. The great present hope for higher education lies in such a raising of high schools in tone, in organization, in equipment as would not only set university education on sound foundations, but would also make the schools themselves a real training ground for life. This is not a fantastic or problematic undertaking, but something definitely attainable at no long-distant time. Several causes combine to make the present time propitious and the outlook hopeful. First there are the influences of university reform, what has already been achieved, and what is in process of achievement. Secondly there is the influence of training colleges.

The Resolution of 1887[1] pressed strongly the need of more serious attention to the training of teachers. "No money," it is said, "is better spent than that allotted to the support of efficient training schools and colleges for teachers, and money is not well spent if granted to schools presided over by untrained and incompetent teachers, in which discipline and moral training are relegated to a secondary place. The Governor-General in Council is of opinion that in the truest interests of education the cost of providing thoroughly good training

[1] See below, p. 81.

schools and colleges for teachers of English as well as of vernacular schools should be regarded as a first charge on the educational grant and that any province which is now unprovided with institutions suitable for the effectual training of the various classes of teachers required should take measures by retrenchment, if necessary, to establish the requisite training institutions." The Commission of 1882 had been content to record the fact that only in Madras was there a separate training college for English teachers. The last few years have seen a great change, and finally, Bengal and Eastern Bengal, following the example of Bombay, have founded colleges in which training for high school work is being carried on with strenuous purpose. If the training colleges are animated with the right spirit, they will send out year by year to high schools throughout the two provinces teachers inspired with high ideals, instructed in the practice of methods capable of revolutionizing the whole system of secondary education. Not least of these is a method of teaching English which has life in it and a potential development of which the full measure has not yet been taken. This is the third great ground of hopefulness. The method of teaching English has been so unspeakably bad in the past that the assured hope of better methods excites the most lively anticipation of an improvement in the acquisition of English out of all proportion to anything hitherto experienced. Such better methods there are, capable of making the acquisition of English a living, not a dead, process, whether they are called by a technical name, or regarded as merely a commonsense development of methods in use from the beginning of language learning. There is a consensus of evidence that, wherever it has been tried, the Direct Method produces results that may fairly be called astonishing, giving in two or three years a practical and real command of English, which is not usually acquired in twice as many years of laborious study with grammars and text-books only. If all those favouring circumstances are now taken advantage of, there is assured expectation of a surprising improvement in Matriculation English in five or six years' time. The ultimate increase of efficiency might be estimated at two or three hundred per cent.: the labour-saving and time-saving might be reckoned in years. For the fulfilment of these hopes what is required is that the effort for the improvement of high school education should not be slackened. Fresh effort must be put forth. The completion of the reform movement of 1901–1906 requires a more thorough sifting and a stronger subvention of high schools than any that has so far been undertaken. Higher education can only be securely built up in the colleges when year by year the foundations are better laid in the schools.

XI

MORAL AND RELIGIOUS EDUCATION

THE critics of State education in India are never weary of pointing out that its fatal defect is the absence of any moral and religious basis. Among those who say this are many whose attitude to educational effort in India is unquestionably friendly. Thus the *Times* correspondent, though guarded and moderate in finding fault, speaks of "the careless diffusion of an artificial system of education based none too firmly on mere intellectualism, and bereft of all moral and religious sanction."[1] Mr. S. M. Mitra, another discerning critic of its weak points, says: "Knowledge has been pursued without any regard for training in the moral virtues or in the development of character."[2] Now these and all similar criticisms, friendly or otherwise, must be admitted to have this much justification that all of us are agreed that the strengthening of character is the most important side of education, and that as yet we are far from satisfied with the degree of certainty we can feel that the education being given in India is effective in shaping character rightly. Yet these criticisms, like all the wise things that have been said about the moral and religious side of education since education was spoken of at all in

[1] Chirol, "Indian Unrest," p. 322.

[2] S. C. Mitra, "Indian Problems," with an Introduction by Sir George Birdwood (Murray, 1908), p. 29.

India, remain mere words, until it has been shown practically how effect is to be given to this desire to give education in India a stronger moral foundation. For, in point of fact, admirable things have been reiterated about the importance of this side of education since quite the early days. Even when Charles Grant in 1797, before ever there was any State education at all, put forward his scheme for spreading the light of knowledge through India by means of English, the aim which he put first was moral improvement on the most comprehensive scale. "We now proceed," he writes, "to the main object of this work—for the sake of which all the preceding topics and discussions have been brought forward—an inquiry into *the means of remedying disorders* which have become inveterate in the state of society among our Asiatic subjects, which destroy their happiness and obstruct every species of improvement among them." He lays stress in particular on the effects of seeing "a pure, complete, and perfect system of morals and of duty enforced by the most awful sanctions and recommended by the most interesting motives." Moral improvement is equally suggested by Lord Minto in 1811 as a reason for the restoration of Oriental learning. "Little doubt can be entertained," says the resolution, "that the prevalence of the crimes of perjury and forgery so frequently noticed in the official records, is in great measure ascribable, both in Mahomedans and Hindus, to the want of instruction in the moral and religious tenets of their respective faiths. It has been even suggested, and apparently not without foundation, that to this uncultivated state of the minds of the natives is in a great degree to be ascribed the prevalence of those crimes which were recently a scourge to the country."

The primary object of the foundation of the Hindu

College was no doubt to impart knowledge, the new knowledge of the West, which gave to Western nations their extraordinary superiority in the practical concerns of life. But David Hare was one of its first founders, and his connection with the college was undoubtedly moral in its nature. The close personal influence of such a man while he lived (he died in 1842) could not be without its effects. Indeed, its effects are living and visible to the present day in that cult of his memory which leads Hindus, alien in race and religion, to meet together on the anniversary of his death to do honour to his virtues and keep green the remembrance of his benefactions. Gratitude is a moral quality, and in this instance it has survived death.

No doubt also Macaulay's enthusiasm is for "intellectual improvement;" and his faith is that the way of improvement lies through the learning of English and the study of European literature. But it would be unfair to suppose that this zeal for pure knowledge and the impetus to educational effort which followed it are divorced from moral ideas. They were, on the contrary, inspired by an essentially moral idea, the idea of a general elevation in civilization. All that may fairly be said in criticism of Macaulay's standpoint is that it was too easily assumed that more accurate knowledge would necessarily bring with it moral improvement and happiness. Yet there was definite moral instruction in Government institutions under the auspices of the General Committee after 1840. In that year Mr. Cameron, then a member of the committee, and from 1842 to 1847 its President, wrote in a Minute on the importance of moral training: "In most countries morality is taught as part of religion. Here we are prevented by the circumstances of the country from teaching morality in that manner. It is, therefore, more incumbent than upon other ministries of public instruction to teach morality in the form of Moral Philosophy." In 1851 Mr. J. F. Thomas, one of the members of the Madras Council of education in a Minute criticizing sharply on many points the existing system, drew special attention to the very want of effective moral education which is fastened upon to-day. "Education without moral culture," he wrote, "is probably as often injurious as beneficial to society; and at all events a system like that at present in force, which to a great degree overlooks this point, and which makes little or no provision for this most essential part of education, is so radically defective that I feel satisfied that although it may be upheld for a time under special and peculiar circumstances, it must in the end fail, and I hold that unless it can be shown that the people of this Presidency are opposed to receiving moral instruction, combined with intellectual, there is no ground for this palpable practical omission in the existing system."

There is no paragraph of the Despatch of 1854 directly bearing on the subject of moral education, but an earlier letter is quoted in support of the encouragement of education as calculated "not only to produce a higher degree of intellectual fitness, but to raise the moral character of those who partake of its advantages;" and a valuable testimony is later given to the actual efficacy of education in producing such effects. The Directors say: "We are sanguine enough to believe that some effect has already been produced by the improved education of the public service in India. The ability and integrity of a large and increasing number of the native judges, to whom the greater part of the civil jurisdiction in India is now committed, and the high estimation in which many among them are held by their fellow-countrymen is, in our opinion, much to be attributed to the progress of education among these officers, and to their adoption along with it of that high moral tone which pervades the general literature of Europe."

The preamble to the Act constituting the universities in January, 1857, says nothing of moral education. The model of the Universities of Calcutta, Madras, and Bombay was the London University, their declared aim was the test of proficiency in study and the affiliated colleges were non-residential. The method of education in the colleges, however, was what it had been before the establishment of universities, and what had been said in 1851 about moral education by the first historian of education in Bengal, Mr. J. Kerr, held good: "Whatever enlarges the mind or refines the taste, tends to improve character. All the studies of our colleges have thus, in a greater or less degree, the effect that is aimed at in a systematic treatise on moral science. If our students remain stunted in moral growth, it is not for want of instruction, which is imparted largely and in most attractive and impressive forms.

The Education Commission of 1882 devoted separate sections to moral and religious training. Their preliminary remarks on the former settle once for all the limits of discussion: "The subject of moral training in colleges is replete with difficulties—difficulties, however, that are mainly practical. For there is no difference of opinion as to moral training being as necessary as intellectual or physical training, and no dissent from the principle that a system in which moral training was wholly neglected would be unworthy of the name of education. Nor, again, is there any difference of opinion as to the moral value of the love of law and order, of the respect for superiors, of the obedience, regularity, and attendance to duty which every well-conducted college is calculated to promote. All these have, by the nearly universal consent of the witnesses, done a great deal to elevate the moral tone and improve the daily practice of the great bulk of those who have been trained in the colleges of India. The degree in which different colleges have exerted a moral influence of this kind is probably as various as the degree of success that has attended the intellectual training given in them and has doubtless been different in all colleges at different times, depending as it does on the character and personal influence of the Principal and Professors who may form the staff at any given period. So far all the witnesses, and probably all intelligent men, are substantially agreed. Difficulties begin when the question is raised whether good can be done by distinct moral teaching over and above the moral supervision which all admit to be good and useful, and which all desire to see made more thorough than it is at present." After a careful review of the conflicting opinions and practice, the Commission made two recommendations on the subject of direct moral instruction: (1) That an attempt be made to prepare a moral text-book based upon the fundamental principles of natural religion, such as may be taught in all Government and non-Government Colleges. (2) That the Principal or one of the Professors in each Government or Aided College deliver to each of the College classes in every session a series of lectures on the duties of a man and a citizen.

These recommendations did not win the acceptance either of the Local or of the Supreme Government and have remained a dead letter. Some arguments used by the Commission in their report go far to remove any regret that might be felt on this account. They say: "In all colleges and under all courses of instruction the most effective moral training consists in inculcating habits of order, diligence, truthfulness, and due self-respect combined with submission to authority, all of which lessons a good teacher finds useful opportunities of imparting. The formation of such habits is promoted by the study of the lives and actions of great men, such as the student finds in the course of his English reading; and it may be hoped, by the silent influence upon his character of constant intercourse with teachers, whom he is able to regard with respect and affection. Nor, again, is there reason to believe that collegiate education of the present type has any injurious effect upon the life and character of students. On the contrary, the nearly unanimous testimony of those who have had the best opportunities of observing goes to show that in integrity, in self-respect, in stability of purpose, and generally in those solid qualities which constitute an honourable and useful character, the University graduate is generally superior to those who have not enjoyed the advantages which college training confers."

As regards direct religious teaching the Commission of 1882 report with no uncertain voice its impracticability. Government institutions cannot undertake such teaching owing to Government's declared policy of religious neutrality. The Commission weigh carefully the complaints that have been made of the demoralizing influence of the exclusion of religion. They consider the remedy proposed "that Government should employ teachers of all prevalent forms of religion to give instruction in its colleges, or should at least give such teachers admission to its colleges if their services are provided by outside bodies." They conclude: "We are unable to recommend any plan of this kind." However praiseworthy the feelings that underlie such a proposal, "we are satisfied that no such scheme can be reduced to practice in the present state of Indian society."

It cannot be said that the subject of moral education has been neglected. If anything is wanting it is supplied by a resolution of the Government of India in 1887 directed wholly to enforcing the necessity of careful attention to school and college discipline. "The question of discipline in schools and colleges," it premises, "does not seem to have hitherto received any comprehensive consideration apart from the discussion of the subject by the Education Commission;" and it acknowledges that "the growth of tendencies unfavourable to discipline and favourable to irreverence has accompanied the general extension of education." It advocates the firm maintenance of discipline in Indian schools and colleges, based on the standard recognized in the highest schools and colleges in England which nowadays does not err on the side of severity. It then deals at length with the problem of discipline in schools, discerningly pointing out that, if right habits of discipline are formed in schools, the problem of collegiate discipline is materially simplified. Among the suggestions for schools are the introduction of the monitorial system, the building of boarding-houses, well-defined rules; and the value of training for teachers is especially insisted on. For colleges the su gestions are of weekly college meetings and recognized disciplinary powers (fines, suspension, rustication, expulsion) for both Principals and Professors. The value of the encouragement of physical exercise is emphasized, and teaching having a direct bearing upon conduct is recommended. The resolution concludes with an emphatic affirmation of the importance of the subject. "In conclusion I am to commend the whole subject to early and careful attention, for the importance of the considerations thus brought to notice cannot be exaggerated. The true interests of education are bound up with the solution of the problems now touched upon."

It would appear from all this that the importance of the moral side of education has by no means been overlooked in the sixty years that have passed since the despatch of 1854 formally adopted English education. If, as we have seen, there has been a steadily deepening sense of responsibility for the moral side of education in the policy of the Government of India, as evidenced by authoritative documents, and yet well-meant criticism continues to show that we have little ground to congratulate ourselves on the success achieved, the cause of failure must be sought otherwhere than in want of attention to the subject. A suspicion may take shape that the impediment lies in the nature of the task attempted. The education of character, which is presumably what is meant by moral education, is something very deep-lying, and depends on a number of factors of which school life is only one. Now it is not very difficult to put together a number of common-places on the importance of moral education. It may in some circumstances be exceedingly difficult to turn precept into practice. The thing to be done is so to train boys that they may grow up to be manly, truth-loving, courageous, law-abiding, with just notions of self-respect and of what is due to others. It is by no means easy anywhere to bring this to pass through the daily routine work of school and college, and in India there are hindrances of a very baffling nature. In any case the burden is laid upon the professed teacher in school and college. He it is who must bear the responsibility and do the work, if it can be done. It may be well then to listen to the comments of one whose profession is education on the last and most pointed government utterance on the subject, the very judicious circular of 1887.

"I would respectfully beg leave to say a word or two with respect to the causal connection assumed in the letter of the Government of India to exist between the education imparted in our schools and colleges, and 'the growth of tendencies unfavourable to discipline and favourable to irreverence in the rising generation.' No one could be more sensible than I am of the imperfections of our educational system, but I cannot believe that schools and colleges have been largely instrumental in bringing about the state of things complained of. I consider, on the contrary, that we teachers have cause to complain that the tone of our schools has been prejudicially affected by the tendencies unfavourable to authority invading them from without . . . Indian society is breathing the same social and political atmosphere as all other civilized communities—an atmosphere which happens at present to be deficient in reverence for authority and in willingness to submit to it. Are the seeds of these tendencies sown in our schools and colleges and fostered and made to fructify there? I think not. Beyond what naturally follows from that emancipation of thought which is one of the first-fruits of a liberal education everywhere, I do not believe that the system of education pursued in India has had any hand in fostering 'the growth of tendencies unfavourable to discipline and favourable to irreverence.' My contentions that these tendencies belong to the world that lies outside our schools and colleges, that they colour the thoughts and feelings and aspirations of the grown-up generation, and that from this outside world they invade our schools and infect our pupils—these contentions are borne out by the two following considerations: first, that it was not till after the political and racial excitement of recent years had spread throughout India that the youth attending schools and colleges showed signs of turbulence and insubordination; and secondly, that these tendencies were practically confined to those provinces in the north of India where political and racial feelings were most bitter. In the Madras Presidency, where the feelings never ran very high, our educational institutions have hitherto enjoyed an almost absolute immunity from such disturbances; and to the honour of the students of this college, be it said, there has not, during the eighteen years I have been connected with them, been any other disposition manifested than that of cheerful and loyal obedience to the rules of the institution."

This commentary shows the whole question of the relation of the political and educational movements in a new aspect. Is it possible that cause and effect are being confused, when education is blamed, and that it is not the educational system which has produced political disaffection, but disaffection towards the existing order, otherwise generated, has first produced its effects in society at large, then invaded and injuriously affected the educational system. The relations of cause and effect are in a complicated material hard to disentangle, and where interaction is a necessary factor in the problem, mistake as to the ultimate causation is easily made. But the question here is not of the causes of "unrest," but of the means of improving the moral influence of education. The writer of the memorandum from which the above quotation is made was Dr. Duncan, at the time Principal of the Presidency College, Madras, and afterwards for many years Director of Public Instruction in the Madras Presidency. His opinion in the matter is entitled to great weight, and what he further says on the subject may help to determine just conclusions on the difficult question of moral and religious education in Indian colleges and schools. Judgment of what has been done in the past and of what may be better done in the future depends closely on just conclusions as to what is *possible*.

I will take first the question of religious education. When I see religious education seriously advocated as the basis of morality in Indian schools and colleges, I wonder if those who advocate it have any clear ideas as to what they mean. Which religion? In India there are many religions. "Have there not been, are there not religious beliefs utterly antagonistic to genuine morality? In spite of this people speak and write as if the problem of moral education would be solved were religious instruction provided for the young! It surely ought to be recognized that everything will depend on the moral character of the religious beliefs inculcated. No one would recommend the teaching of any and every religious dogma in Indian schools; and until such beliefs as may on moral grounds be taught, are separated from such as may not be taught, the question of religious instruction must remain one on which no practical policy can be adopted." Dr. Duncan wrote thus in 1888. Now twenty years later the voices protesting the inadequacy of secular education and the indispensable necessity of religious education are many and powerful. Sir Andrew Fraser writes in October last in the *Nineteenth Century* "we want a higher type of education, a system that recognizes the moral and religious side of a man's training as well as the intellectual and physical." "The genius of Indian thought, the demands of Indian parents, the strong representation of Indian chiefs are all in favour of religious education."[1] Bishop Welldon, who knows a little of India and much of education, is reported a few weeks ago as declaring that he held with an intensity of conviction which it was difficult to express "that secular education, wherever it was given, and by whomsoever it was given, was a lamentable failure." If one is seriously desirous of amending what is amiss with the educational system in India such utterances as these must give him pause. There is also something plausible and persuasive in the argument, especially when it follows on the failure, or assumed failure, of moral education without religion. Still one does not readily, perhaps, shake oneself free of the old prepossession that religious teaching is impossible in conjunction with modern education in India, which seemed so short a while ago a maxim universally accepted. At any rate we are entitled to inquire by what particular instrumentality it is to be done; done rightly; and done safely. For we have been apt to look upon religion in India as somewhat like a powder magazine, to be approached cautiously. Certainly there are difficulties. Illustrations quite remote from India will help to their clearer apprehension. Could we be content to found our school morality on the worship of Thor and Odin, of Hela and the Valkyries? Could we cheerfully revive in our colleges the many coloured polytheism of Greece and Rome? We should acknowledge there were elements of good in the religion of Hellas. There were also evil elements against which Plato and the philosophers inveighed before ever the

[1] "Indian Unrest," by Sir Andrew Fraser. *Nineteenth Century* for October, 1910, p. 753.

zeal of the early Christians turned the gods of Greece into demons. There was the worship of Dionysus and Aphrodite as well as of Apollo and of Pallas Athene. In some cults human sacrifice survived. The thief, the murderer, and the adulterer all found their patron deity to pray to. In India, too, there are many and divers cults, and there is at all events danger of reviving religious cults in favour of evil morals rather than good. The problem is too hard for us. We take refuge in toleration. We tolerate all religions in colleges, so long as they do not actively propagate crime: we give free opportunity to religious teachers outside the guarded sphere of scholastic training. We do not actively assist religious teaching within it, because we are debarred from exercising any discrimination as to what we judge good or ill. We cannot secure that only the good shall come in: so we think it safer to admit none at all.

There is a practical difficulty remaining also, if we should determine to make the experiment of aiding and abetting direct religious instruction. So far as colleges were intended to represent one religion only, like the Sanskrit College or Alighar, there would not be (as there is not now) any difficulty. But it is not practicable, even were it desirable, to make all schools and colleges sectarian. How can religious teaching be introduced, if the school or college authorities do not themselves take the responsibility for it? Only by admitting teachers from outside. This, however, gives rise to an objection which to the man who works in school or college is probably decisive: it would be to introduce rival authorities into college and school, the educational and the religious. There would be too great apprehension that this rival authority might undermine discipline for the teacher ever to acquiesce in it with an easy mind.

It is not possible to discuss the subject exhaustively, and more might doubtless be said on both sides. The balance appears to the present writer to be decisively against the expediency of making a radical change in the policy hitherto followed by the Government of India in regard to religious education.

It remains, then, that our education of character, so far as schools and colleges are concerned, must be independent of a specially religious basis. This does not, however, at all necessarily mean that it is cut off from all appeal to what is most morally persuasive in religion. The true essence of belief, as far as morals are concerned, is that God is on the side of righteousness. This it is which gives effective power to religion as a motive to morality. The appeal to this fundamental faith is not denied to the teacher on a purely secular basis of education. This belief involves no theological dogma and offends no religious susceptibilities. The appeal is, therefore, always within the secular teacher's discretion.

For the rest our task must be to make the best of the ordinary means of moral education: and the only practical question here is whether any means have been overlooked which might be employed; is there anything more which might be done now? "Morality," Dr. Duncan well says, "must be taught in schools in the way in which it is taught at home, and in the social life of the young. Morality cannot be taught as a branch of knowledge forming part of the school curriculum, nor is a special text-book the best means of inculcating it. That danger of neglecting the spirit for the letter, which has to be particularly guarded against, when text-books are used in teaching the ordinary branches of knowledge, would be much more menacing were the attempt made to teach morality through a specially prepared text-book." This is well said and decisive against one of the two practical suggestions of the Commission of 1882. The second was for series of lectures on the duties of a man and a citizen. Now it is very certain that college addresses by the principal of a college to the college as a whole are very necessary as an incentive and support of the corporate life of a college. They should, however, deal with the duties of the members of a collegiate society rather than duties of members of the community in a wider sense. Such addresses should be made to students as students of the college (and of that college in particular), and should bear closely on the particular and present circumstances of life in the college. They should, in a broad sense, be lay sermons. A principal who is not full to overflowing with thoughts for such addresses can have very imperfectly realized the obligations and privileges of his position. If in particular cases, and for exceptional reasons, a principal feels unable to take on himself this responsibility, he may delegate the function to such members of the college staff as are fitted to discharge it. There is some loss of efficacy if the head of the college speaks by deputy, but the essential point is that there should be regular addresses, and that these addresses should concern themselves with the students' present surroundings and responsibilities. If the student learns aright the lesson of his duties as a student, there will be no question later on as to his recognition of what is due from him as a man and a citizen. Addresses need not be very frequent, better not. Once or twice in a year should suffice; but there can be no hard-and-fast line drawn in the matter. Along with such direct and solemn incentives to right doing, the most potent instrument of moral *education* is, undoubtedly, good rules of discipline, considerately imposed and firmly enforced. The habit of obedience to rule has formal value in itself; willing obedience to good rules with a recognition that they are good is moral education of the most effective kind. In the main character must be formed by action; right actions from right motives trained into virtuous habits. As Dr. Duncan writes:—"Practical morality is an art which is learnt like every other art, solely by doing moral actions." Hence the preponderant value of well-regulated school and college discipline. Yet even that cannot be fully efficacious of itself. So much depends also on the nature which the pupil brings for school discipline to mould and on the influences of his other surroundings, his earliest associations, his out-of-school companions, his home. These things cannot be regulated by the teacher: they lie almost absolutely outside the reach of his influence; and these outside influences are by no means always favourable. All the more pressing is his responsibility and the need for increasing the efficacy of moral teaching in the school.

Undoubtedly the most important factor of all is the character of the teacher himself. And here again Government policy has not failed, but is on the right lines. "The Government of India," says Dr. Duncan, "have rightly given the foremost place among their recommendations to the employment of trained teachers and the provision of efficient training schools"; and he is able to point with satisfaction to the attention which had already at that date been paid to the subject in Madras. Bengal, on the other hand, has lagged behind and is endeavouring with the happiest promise to make up ground now. The extreme importance of right selection of teachers in every grade, and especially in the highest, is not yet sufficiently recognized, at any rate not sufficiently provided for. In the matter of discipline also the support the teacher may count on getting might be made more assured. The enforcement of judicious rules is, as has been said, the chief educational instrument. There must be no doubt that the fearless enforcement of discipline by the teacher will receive support, if support is needed. This has not always been sufficiently well assured in the past. If these two things are better done: (1) unsparing effort made to secure that teachers shall be men of high character; (2) due provision made for establishing and maintaining sound discipline, Government will have done all that is at present possible for moral education. No radical change of policy is called for; only the better and more efficient carrying out of the policy long since adopted.

XII

MASS EDUCATION

THERE can be no doubt that the Despatch of 1854 contemplated a general extension of popular education, and desired in particular to bring education to those classes "who are utterly incapable of obtaining any education worthy of the name by their own unaided efforts." But when the Commission of 1882 flatly recommended "That primary education be declared to be that part of the whole system of Public Instruction which possesses an almost exclusive claim on local funds set apart for education and a large claim on provincial revenues," they went far beyond anything in the Despatch of 1854. In the Despatch of 1854 it will be found that primary and secondary schools are dealt with together in the same paragraphs as parts of the one problem of popular education. "Schools—whose objects should be not to train a few youths but to provide more opportunities than now exist for the acquisition of such an improved education as will make those who possess it more useful members of society in every condition of life—should exist in every district in India. . . ." "We include in this class of institutions those which, like the Zillah Schools of Bengal, the district Government Anglo-Vernacular Schools of Bombay, and such as have been established by the Raja of Burdwan and other native gentlemen in different parts of India, use the English language as the chief medium of instruction; as well as others of an inferior order, such as the Tahsili schools in the North-West Provinces, and the Government Vernacular schools in the Bombay Presidency. . . ." "Lastly, what have been called indigenous schools should by wise encouragement . . . be made capable of imparting correct elementary knowledge to the great mass of the people." All classes of schools were to be encouraged by the new system of grants-in-aid, and it is specifically laid down that grants should as a general principle "be made to such schools . . . as require some fee, however small, from their scholars." The Commission of 1882 still contemplated the levying of fees in aided schools as a general rule, but advocated the admission of free students on the ground of poverty and "a general or larger exemption in the case of special schools established for the benefit of poorer classes."

The overwhelming verity in respect of primary education is the immense scale of the problem. In 1885 Sir C. P. Ilbert, after recalling the great advance between 1853 and 1882, adds: "And yet, after all these figures the stern fact remains that education has succeeded in reaching only some ten per cent. of the male population of India and has scarcely reached the female population at all." His conclusion is: "The task of the future is gigantic but not impracticable." A quarter of a century has passed since he wrote, and the latest statistics available show that whereas the total number of boys who should be at school in primary schools proportionately to the population of India is eighteen millions, the number actually at school is rather over three and a half millions, or a fifth of the whole. The actual total for 1885 is somewhat under two millions and a half, so that the advance of twenty-five years is one million two hundred thousand. The figure for male literacy by the census of 1901 is 102 per thousand, or practically still 10 per cent. It cannot be contended that these facts and figures afford much ground for satisfaction.

The resolution of March the 11th, 1904, the latest formal statement of the Government of India's educational policy, reaffirms the great need of primary education and acknowledges the obligation for more attention to it. The conclusion to which Government is brought in Section 18 is "that primary education has hitherto received insufficient attention and an inadequate share of the public funds. They consider that it possesses a strong claim upon the sympathy of the Supreme Government and of the Local Government, and should be made a leading charge upon Provincial revenues; and that in those provinces where it is in a backward condition, its encouragement should be a primary obligation." As regards aims and policy, then, there has been consistency of statement and a growth in the intensive perception of the responsibility involved from 1854 to 1904. But recognition of the greatness of the problem and affirmation of the duty of accepting responsibility for it, though valuable as incitements to effort, leave things just as they were, until words and intentions take shape in action. What action has been taken? What action is possible? These are the practical problems. Something has been done since 1901. Primary education had a share in the Imperial grant of 40 lakhs to education in 1902. Thirty-five lakhs have been given exclusively to primary education from Imperial revenues since 1905. Between 1902 and 1907 schools have increased by 10,700; scholars by 622,000. This is something substantial, and all the more significant that progress between 1892 and

1902 is hardly appreciable. But this half million or so of boys is itself but a small fraction compared with fourteen million still to be reached. Mr. Orange says: "If the number of boys at school continued to increase even at the rate of increase that has taken place in the last five years, and there were no increase of population, several generations would still elapse before primary education can be universally diffused." In face of the vast area of the problem still untouched, the contrast between what has been done and the doctrine of free compulsory education is grotesque. On any plain reading of facts and possibilities compulsory education is beyond the horizon and free education on any comprehensive scale of doubtful expediency. The reasons why beyond a certain point, which possibly has already been almost reached, the extension of popular education must of necessity be increasingly difficult, were cogently stated by Mr. Nathan in the review of 1902. "The main cause," he writes, "is no doubt that numerical progress must be made downwards, and that every step down is attended by greater and greater difficulty and expense. When the Education Departments began to devote their attention to the general furtherance of primary instruction, they had in the first place to deal with a portion of the population who were accustomed to and valued education and who lived in populous and easily accessible parts of the country; and they were aided by a more or less widespread system of indigenous schools. In such circumstances progress was comparatively easy. These favourable conditions have now been to a great extent exhausted, and the portion of the problem which remains to be dealt with is far harder. The benefits of education have now to be conveyed to the poorer raiyats, the lower castes and the wilder tribes who have from time immemorial lived without instruction. . . . In many cases the illiterate portion of the population lives in scattered villages and in parts of the country in which the means of communication are still indifferent. To establish small schools in such localities for an indifferent or unwilling population cannot fail to be a difficult and expensive task." There is obviously a just perception of hard realities in this statement of causes, though it is far from excluding a large, a very large, practical demand for new schools if only money were forthcoming. But not only has the area over which primary education has still to spread to be considered, but, unless all the lessons of the past are to go for nothing, the quality of primary education has to be well considered also before any forward movement on an extraordinary scale is further planned. Several considerations offer here; and while signs of good comfort are not wanting, there is much which calls for deliberation and caution. School buildings have to be considered, equipment, plans of education and, above all, teachers. On all these heads, and especially the last, there is much to give the "impatient idealist" pause. No great forward movement is practicable without a greatly reinforced army of teachers; no forward movement will be of real avail without an army of trained teachers. Efforts are being made to train teachers in every province of the Empire, and considerable success is being achieved. But what has been done does not by a long interval suffice for the adequate officering of the schools which already exist; there is no great reserve from which battalions for fresh conquests can be drawn. Long continued and ever more determined effort is needed and the lapse of many years before there can by any possibility be a multitude of duly trained teachers to be sent forth to occupy new territories. If there is one point clearly brought out by the last quinquennial review, by the Resolution of 1904, by provincial reports on public instruction since 1907, especially those for Bengal, it is the inadequate payment of primary school teachers and the imperative necessity of making the teacher's livelihood better and better assured, if there is to be any advance of popular education worth the name.

This is the consideration of dominant importance, and to this, if the intention to throw greater energy into the organization and spread of primary education is real, attention must be paid in the first place—even before the provision of training schools, absolutely essential as the training of teachers is to success. It is known that in Bengal at all events the agency for training elementary teachers, inadequate as it is, has already outgrown the effective demand which the actual prospects of teachers make on the pupils of training schools. Inspectors report that too frequently teachers are trained at public expense in guru-training schools and then betake themselves to callings less ill-remunerated than that of the village schoolmaster. This question of the provision of qualified teachers is so much the most important that all other requirements of primary education sink into insignificance compared with it. And yet the provision of schools and of suitable equipment for schools are problems of great scale and some difficulty. In the planning of suitable courses of instruction great progress has been made, and this is the most promising factor in the problem. Common sense has at last effected the adoption of courses which have a practical and intimate relation to the life of the classes for whose benefit they are instituted. There is great hope here. When the teachers are added to the courses of instruction, the most important conditions will have been secured for a great and memorable advance, which will only then be further limited by the extent to which Imperial and local funds can be provided.

There is not and cannot be any question of checking any effort which the new Department or Local Governments may make in the immediate future for the improvement and expansion of mass education. Only out of the experience of the past fifty years certain lessons should be laid to heart, and these prescribe caution. Two cautions in particular would seem to be timely. One is not to let go any vantage that has accrued from educational effort since 1857, and, in particular, the gains, at present insecure and only beginning to be realized, of the educational movement from 1901 to 1906. The other is less welcome to a sincere faith in the efficacy of education and in the grandeur of the design outlined by the authors of the Despatch of 1854 and of the other great documents which define the policy of the Government of India, but none the less necessary to state. It is this. The success of the great expansion of higher education since 1857, and more specially since 1882, though not in the main to be doubted, is not in all aspects so clear and undoubted that we can go on lightheartedly to take in hand a problem of far vaster magnitude and of potentialities even more deeply hidden from our ken. Some of the results of higher education have been unanticipated and have taken its well-wishers by surprise. We did not know what the economic results of higher education would be; we did not know what the political results would be. Are we sure we can gauge all the consequences of universal mass education, and that, if we could, we should welcome them all? English education had surprises in store alike for pedagogue and statesman. Is it possible that universal popular education might have some also? There is reason for greatly enhanced effort. There is reason for hopefulness and enthusiasm and zeal. There is justification for all and more than all that the new Department and all the Local Governments can do. But there is reason also for caution against haste to expand, to see results, to quote statistics. Nothing useful can be accomplished solely by sweeping ordinances from headquarters and the announcement of a grandiose programme. If good is to be done, it will be done by the quiet effort of myriads of humble workers, inspired and patiently organized by educational captains. A chastened recognition of the greatness of the task to be undertaken and of the insufficiency of the means, unless by persistent hopefulness and unfaltering zeal they are multiplied and intensified into adequacy, must go before any effective advance on the great scale. It is perseverance and indomitable renewal of effort, steady and gradually enlarged development of the agencies at work, that are needed, not any striking new departure.

XIII

THE EDUCATION DEPARTMENTS AND THEIR WORK

"In the selection of the heads of the educational departments, the inspectors and other officers, it will be of the greatest importance to secure the services of persons who are not only best able from their character, position, and acquirements, to carry our objects into effect, but who may command the confidence of the natives of India. It may, perhaps, be advisable that the first heads of the Educational Department, as well as some of the inspectors, should be members of our civil service; as such appointments in the first instance would tend to raise the estimation in which these officers will be held, and to show the importance we attach to the subject of education, and also as amongst them you will probably find the persons best qualified for the performance of the duty."

In these words the Despatch of 1854 strikes the right key-note, the paramount importance in education of selecting the right men. In reviewing the work of the departments it will be well to give the foremost place to this aspect of organization, because apart from men to work it, machinery is of little avail. I shall examine, then, what steps were originally taken to give effect to this cardinal principle, and how it has since been safeguarded.

The earliest appointed Directors of Public Instruction in accordance with the suggestion of the despatch were members of the Indian Civil Service; in Bengal, Mr. Gordon Young (described by Sir Alexander Arbuthnot in "Memories of Rugby and India" as a man of imposing physique[1]); in Bombay, Mr. J. C. Erskine (a little later Vice-Chancellor of Calcutta University); in Madras, Mr. A. J. Arbuthnot, whose memoirs, published last year, have just been referred to. But it was not intended to make education a branch of the existing civil service. It was eventually to be independently administered by men specially qualified for educational work. The despatch continues: "But we desire that neither these offices, nor any other connected with education, shall be considered as necessarily to be filled by members of that service, to the exclusion of others, Europeans or Natives, who may be better fitted for them; and that in any case the scale of their remuneration shall be so fixed as publicly to recognize the important duties they will have to perform." These points are emphasised in a supplementary despatch dated April 7th, 1859. It is added: "The spirit of the instructions of the Court of Directors with regard to the classes from whom the officers of the department were to be selected appears to have been duly observed. In Bengal, the North-Western Provinces, Madras, and Bombay, members of the civil service were in the first instance appointed Directors of Public Instruction; and the several appointments of Inspectors were filled indiscriminately by civil servants, military and medical officers, and individuals unconnected with any of these services. In the Punjab, the office of Director has

[1] "The latter (Mr. Gordon Young) was a very agreeable, and, as far as I could judge, an extremely able man, immensely tall and broad in proportion," pp. 113, 114.

from the first been held by a gentleman who was at the time of his nomination in the military service, but who retired from the army immediately on appointment. In Bombay the first Director, Mr. Erskine, has been succeeded by a gentleman who was previously a barrister; and among the present Inspectors it is believed that there are not in all the Presidencies more than two or three members of the civil service."

So far there is no explicit recognition of the fact that there is, or might be, a distinct educational profession for which special qualifications and training are required, as distinct from those of military, medical, and administrative officers, or practising barristers, and that gentlemen appointed to an *Education* Department should by preference have these qualifications; but it seems to be glanced at later on in this despatch, where it is written: "After a full consideration of the grounds on which the Court of Directors formerly gave their sanction as a temporary arrangement to the employment of covenanted civil servants in the Department of Education, Her Majesty's Government are, on the whole, of opinion that as a general rule all appointments in the Department of Education should be filled by individuals unconnected with the service of Government either civil or military. It is not their wish that officers now in the department should be disturbed for the sole purpose of carrying out this rule; and they are aware that difficulty might at present be experienced in finding well qualified persons, unconnected with the regular services, to fill vacant offices in the department. But it is their desire that the rule now prescribed be kept steadily in view, and that every encouragement be given to *persons of education* to enter the educational service, even in the lower grades, by making it known that in the nominations to the higher offices in the department preference will hereafter be given to those who may so enter it, if competent to discharge the duties." The reasons for this policy are stated somewhat more trenchantly by Sir G. R. Clerk, at the time an Under-Secretary of State, in a memorandum dated March 29, 1858. Among other suggestions and criticisms he urges it as advisable "To discontinue the practice of appointing civilians or others properly belonging to the civil or military administration to conduct any of the departments of education. When so engaged they are themselves in a transition state. They are looking for promotion in departments quite unconnected with education. They are therefore eager for immediate distinction in the sphere in which they find themselves temporarily placed."

A separate educational service was accordingly formed parallel with the Civil, Medical, Opium, Jail, Police, Customs and other branches of administration under the several provincial governments. This higher service was subsequently after reorganization and improvement known as the Graded Educational Service; and after 1896 as the Indian Educational Service, and since leadership and guidance in the actual field of education have necessarily been committed to the men appointed to this service, the conditions of service and the quality of the men attracted to it were matters of the deepest moment. A curious complication of the problem of selection has been that in India the education departments have discharged a function usually performed by distinct agency, the staffing of colleges doing university work. In Germany university professors are appointed by Government, and receive their salaries from the State, but they are not, so far as I am aware, graded in a list which includes also school inspectors. In the United Kingdom the State Education

Department is concerned only with school education, and for the most part primary school education. The significant difference is best brought out by saying that in England till recently the Education Department had nothing to do with secondary education, and has comparatively little even now, and that it has never had anything at all to do with university education. In India collegiate education was an important branch of the work of the education departments—even the most important in proportion as the bias since 1835, and still more since 1857, has lent to the side of university education. After 1855 the *staffing* of Government colleges in a province was the business of the provincial education department. Principals and professors of colleges, as well as inspectors of schools, were recruited for and graded in a single service. This may not have been felt as an embarrassment from the beginning; but it became so as soon as the departmental system came fully into operation, and questions of promotion and of transfer from one appointment to another arose. Even this produced no great inconvenience in the earlier years, though a professor of Mathematics or Botany might next year find himself an inspector of schools, or one appointed for his qualifications in Philosophy or History be required a little later to teach English literature, because work was little specialized in the colleges, and it was not till later that any great importance was attached to special training to fit the school inspector for his work. When, however, the work of the colleges became more advanced with the institution of Honour and M.A. courses of study, serious inconveniences arose and have become more and more sensibly felt; and, finally, definite protests have been raised against them with growing emphasis in the last twenty years. Also as the studies of the colleges became more advanced and more specialized, men with more special qualifications were brought out from time to time direct from the English universities to teach Chemistry or Physics, Mathematics or Philosophy, History or Economics, though it is only quite recently that the conviction that any Englishman (Scotchman or Irishman) of moderate education could teach English literature has begun to give ground. The inconvenience, when the conditions were fully matured, of combining in a homogeneous service functions markedly heterogeneous, is sufficiently obvious. For an inspector of schools you want common sense and administrative capacity coupled with zeal for and belief in education, and such an intimate knowledge of schools as would make him thoroughly master of all the details of their practical organization and working. In a college professor you want first and foremost a competent knowledge of his subject and ability to teach it. A college professor must be a learned man, and a specialist in a particular branch of knowledge. In an inspector of schools you want primarily practical capacity and bodily activity combined with a good general education. These differences are well recognized now in Bengal, and the higher educational service is practically divided into two branches, the collegiate supplying professors equipped with special knowledge of literature and science for colleges; the administrative consisting of divisional inspectors of schools. But relics of the anomaly survive, inasmuch as these two kinds of "officers" are gazetted in the same list, and there is nothing to prevent an interchange of appointments when departmental convenience suggests it. This confusion of functions may fairly, I think, be set down as a defect in the organization of the education departments. It is hardly perhaps to be called an original mistake, because in the fifties the difficulties of recruitment were greater, there was little relevant experience for guidance as to method, and the ill effects of the confusion were not at once apparent, because, as I have said, the work was not as yet really specialized, and one man was within limits equally well-fitted for a variety of functions. It is a defect now, and has been for a long time, and it might have been sooner amended. The same confusion is found in what are now known as the Provincial Educational Services, and in the subordinate branches called respectively the Subordinate and Lower Subordinate Educational Services. In the Provincial Service are found, as in the Indian Service, principals and professors of colleges, demonstrators in science, headmasters and inspectors of schools; and, in addition, translators to Government and incumbents of other anomalous posts. In the Subordinate and Lower Subordinate Services are graded promiscuously head and assistant masters, subordinate inspecting officers, gymnastic instructors, librarians, members of the various clerical establishments, store-keepers, circle pandits, master-blacksmiths, and reformatory guards and escorting officers. The suspicion is generated and grows, whether the departmental system on this comprehensive scale is suited for educational work, unless at all events classes of work are first carefully distinguished; and stronger suspicion takes definite shape, whether the departmental system is suitable at all for colleges; whether a college should not rather be recruited for and equipped solely *ad hoc* (as Sir Alexander Grant actually proposed in 1867) every man in his appointed place and with his special work, and with distinct and appropriate prospects in that work. Startling at first as such a proposition may be to minds familiar with the departmental basis of organization, the impracticability will be found to dwindle when steadily looked in the face, and may even fade away altogether when it is remembered that practically every college in England and most secondary schools are organized on the rival principle. It is not suggested that any wide change would be practicable or expedient, but the drawbacks incidental to a departmental system might with advantage be recognized, and watched; and the endeavour to lessen the disadvantages be consistently maintained.

It now falls to be considered more particularly how in the recruitment of men for the higher educational service effect was given in practice to the policy of the despatch of 1859 to attract to it men specially qualified for educational work, and so to fix the remuneration offered as "publicly to recognize the important duties they will have to perform." It is, however, advisable to reserve this inquiry for separate treatment.

XIV

THE HIGHER EDUCATIONAL SERVICE

WHEN colleges for more advanced education in English were first started in India, no little difficulty was naturally experienced in staffing them. They were at first staffed locally, as we should now say; that is, the least unsuitable men who could be found ready at hand were appointed. Obviously there was no specially literate class of Englishman in India previous to 1854. Even the Haileybury men, however high their intellectual capacity, were not academically educated, and were not pre-eminently scholars. Moreover, as we have seen, members of the Civil Service were implicitly excluded by the Despatch of 1854 from the work of the education departments after the first few years, and I am not aware that a single member of that service was ever a college principal or professor.

From what material, then, could selection be made? An examination of the earliest appointments will show. It will show also that if there was ever a qualified teacher among them it was by accident.

At the Hindu College the teaching staff was originally Indian, but one of the two secretaries was a European "appointed for the special purpose of superintending the English department." The suggestion that it might be necessary to bring teachers from England appears first in 1823 in connection with the teaching of natural science, or, as it was then called, natural philosophy. Five hundred pounds was spoken of as "the lowest sum likely to attract a well-qualified individual to India." The General Committee commented in 1825 on the want of well-qualified instructors: "In order to afford to the students of the Hindu College that full and comprehensive instruction that was desirable, persons duly qualified for the office must be brought from England." "The General Committee considered it of importance that those gentlemen who might be brought out from England should have received a Collegiate education; that they should be laymen, so as to afford no possible ground for misinterpreting the motives of Government; and that they should be persons of extensive acquirements, and capable of communicating as well as accumulating knowledge." The proposal was for two professors so appointed, a Professor of Mathematics and a Professor of English Literature, and particular consideration was given to the qualifications required in the latter. The Committee pointed out that whereas no special qualifications were wanted for teaching Mathematics in India beyond those needed for such work in England, "a teacher of English literature would be placed in a situation to which there was nothing analogous at Home." They added that as it was of great moment to inspire a feeling of interest in our national literature "the preceptor in this department should be imbued with its spirit, and should be a man of taste as well as of letters. He should not only be well read in English authors of different periods, but familiar with their merits, and be able to teach them so that they shall be felt as well as understood." All this was admirably well considered. No professor was appointed from England till 1841 when "two gentlemen selected by Dr. Mill and Mr. Macaulay" arrived in India. "Previous to 1839," writes Mr. Kerr in his Review of Public Instruction in the Bengal Presidency (dated 1853), from which the preceding quotations are also made, "the higher situations in the public colleges, including those of Professors, were invariably filled by men who were available on the spot. The Army, more particularly the Medical Service, furnished some valuable officers, and others were selected from the miscellaneous class who came out to push their fortunes in India. As the colleges rose in importance this source of supply became inadequate, and in 1839 Government perceived the necessity of engaging the services of well-educated men in England."

As soon as it was decided to bring men from England for educational work in India the question of remuneration and prospects at once became acute. What would suffice for men whose homes were in India, and whose strictly educational qualifications were negligible, became ridiculously inadequate for men of "distinguished attainments" from Oxford and Cambridge. The Court of Directors took strong ground on the principle that the colleges "should be placed under European superintendence of the most respectable kind, both as to station and acquirements." "It is, however, to be regretted," adds Mr. Kerr, "that Government has not seen fit to adopt the most rational means in its power of attracting talent to the educational service by holding out the inducement of more liberal remuneration." In 1852, when this was written, the salary of Principals of colleges was Rs.600 a month, of a Professor Rs.400 to Rs.500. This scale was the result of arrangements made in 1840. "It must be allowed," writes Mr. Kerr, "that a very great improvement was effected at this time. But the scale of remuneration is still too low. It is essential to the efficiency of the service that there should at least be a few appointments better paid than any which are at present open to us. As it is, there are no high prizes to reward successful exertion. Our prospects are limited to the attainment of a very moderate income, upon which we live in comfort so long as we enjoy uninterrupted health, but which does not except in the most favourable circumstances, enable us to make any provision for our families, or to retire to our native land."

It is not without relevance to the present to note the exact circumstances of these small beginnings and of the earliest protests of the professional teacher for a more adequate recognition of the importance and worth of his profession. When the Graded Educational Service was organized (about 1870) it afforded something in the shape of the higher prospects, the want of which Mr. Kerr deplored. The initial salary was Rs.500. The highest attainable was Rs.1500. There were four grades, the 4th from Rs.500 to Rs.750; the 3rd from Rs.750 to Rs.1000; the 2nd from Rs.1000 to Rs.1250, and the 1st from Rs.1250 to Rs.1500. In 1896, the service was reorganized under the title of the Indian Educational Service appointed in England. Meanwhile the fall of the rupee had changed relative values much for the worse as compared with earlier times. The range of salaries otherwise remained the same, Rs.500 to Rs.1500. The only change of importance was that instead of waiting for vacancies before promotion from the 4th to the next highest class members of the service are advanced steadily from Rs.500 to Rs.1000 in the first ten years of service. This gives the advantage of regular increase of income, independent of accident.

The prospects beyond ten years were not improved. A very limited number of personal allowances were added, lower allowances of Rs.200 to Rs.250; higher allowances of Rs.250 to Rs.500; and in default of one of these there is an allowance of Rs.100 after fifteen years of approved service. The ordinary limit of the prospects of a member of the Indian Educational Service is Rs.1500 a month, or £1200 a year; and as these higher allowances are very few in number, the average prospects must be rated at something below that.

Two questions can very pertinently be asked from the standpoint of the present: (1) Has the result of these measures been entirely satisfactory? (2) If not, has everything in reason been done to ensure success in this particular? Now as regards the first it happens that a very striking and very public deliverance has recently been made by an observer who must be admitted both competent to pass an opinion and impartial, the author of the *Times* articles on "Indian Unrest." Mr. Valentine Chirol speaks of the Indian Educational Service as "regarded and treated as an inferior branch of the public service."[1] This is at a time when the immense importance of education is reiterated by every responsible representative of Government; and that such a reference could for a moment be made with any plausibility shows that something must be very wrong. It is obligatory then to investigate what has been the mode of recruitment, and what have been the status and attainments of the *personnel* of the higher educational service. In theory appointments to the service, at all events latterly, were made in England: in practice a certain number have always been made in India. A good many of the men appointed were already engaged

[1] Chirol, "Indian Unrest," p. 227.

in educational work in India. Some had come out as missionaries, some as schoolmasters to institutions like the Calcutta Martiniere and the Doveton College, some as tutors to Indian minors of high birth and ample estates. A certain percentage of appointments have always been so made sometimes with very happy results for educational work. Others again have been adventurous pioneers of Oriental scholarship like Blochmann, who took their fortune in their hands, determined only somehow to get to India and gain access to the treasures of learning hidden there. These, rightly valued, have been even the brightest ornaments of the educational service: still, from the purely "Service" standpoint little prestige was brought by any appointment made in India. Spasmodically, however, special pains have been taken to bring out to India from Oxford and Cambridge and other British universities men whose degree qualifications were beyond cavil. There has, therefore, all along been a sprinkling, and ultimately much more than a sprinkling, one way and another, of men whose claims to respect on academic, scientific or literary grounds are indisputable. A scrutiny of the lists of the services between 1855 and the present time reveals not a few names of more than quite local distinction. First among these may be noted Sir Alexander Grant, editor of Aristotle's Ethics, who was Professor and Principal of the Elphinstone Institution from 1860 to 1865, and afterwards Director of Public Instruction. To the Bombay service also belong the great names of Bühler and Kielhorn. In Bengal alone there have been J. W. McCrindle, editor of Arrian, Megasthenes, and other Greek writers about India; Sir Roper Lethbridge, Press Censor in Lord Lytton's time, since well-known in English politics; C. H. Tawney, some time Senior Classic at Cambridge, who has translated *Bharatrihari* and other Sanskrit classics; Sir John Eliot, founder of Meteorological Science in India; C. B. Clarke, the distinguished botanist; Sir Alfred Croft; Sir Alexander Pedler; Dr. C. R. Wilson, whose antiquarian investigations in Calcutta resulted in the exact determination of the site of the Black Hole, and in the two volumes of his "Early Annals of the English in Bengal." Sir Edwin Arnold's name can be added to those of distinguished men on the Bombay side, as he was for some years Principal of the Deccan College. The North-West Provinces have produced several Oriental scholars of high repute, James Ballantyne, Ralph Griffith, A. E. Gough, and Dr. Thibaut. To Bengal again belong Blochmann and Rudolph Hoernle. The first Director in the Punjab was William Delafield Arnold, son of Dr. Arnold of Rugby, and immortalized by his elder brother, Matthew, in "Stanzas from Carnac" and "A Southern Night." The Punjab had till recently in its educational service the explorer, Dr. Stein, who also was at one time in charge of the Calcutta Madrasa. Madras was fortunate in her first Director, Mr. A. J. (afterwards Sir Alexander) Arbuthnot, who was a member of the India Civil Service and returned after some years to general administrative work, but who was essentially a man educationally minded. Other names of distinction in Madras are Mr. E. B. Powell and Dr. Duncan.

These are the more eminent names, taking account only of men no longer on the active list. From the rank and file of the service, whether recruited in England or in India, respectable academic qualifications have always been required, and the picked men have had high academic qualifications. If the service has not that prestige and standing which it is expedient it should have, it does not appear to be from want of a reasonable high standard of academic qualification. There are, however, circumstances which have operated unfavourably, and hindered the educational service from attaining that consideration and influence which the importance of its work and the educational qualifications of its members should rightly carry. Many reasons for this might be suggested, and one of them would be a certain backwardness in pushing their own interests on the part of the members of the service themselves. There are two reasons in special: (1) The educational service necessarily suffers by comparison with the Indian Civil Service, its members being drawn from the same social classes, and having approximately equal qualifications—unless it can be seriously maintained that there is specific virtue in one more competitive examination, and the finish imparted by the crammer's art. (2) The nature of higher educational work is little understood in India: it meets with neither sympathy nor appreciation. If educational work were better understood and proper consideration shown to those engaged upon it on this account, as is to a certain extent the case in England, where a teacher is sometimes esteemed a person entitled to more respect than a man with twice the salary and holding official rank, the disproportion in pay and prospects would matter less. Since, however, the peculiarly delicate and responsible nature of educational work is not socially recognized, and the only standard of value accepted is salary and prospects, the less advantageous terms on which "education" men work, results in a real lowering in public esteem, and this disparagement has undoubtedly exercised a somewhat depressing effect on the atmosphere of educational work.

It might well be deemed a concern for statesmanship

to inquire what steps are necessary in order to assure to the educational service such a heightening of tone and energy as might invigorate the work to the utmost. Two directions of inquiry may be suggested: (1) Supposing the intention to be to secure the steady recruitment of men of exceptional ability, are the terms offered adequate? (2) Are all possible means used—have they been used in the past, to make the nature and interest of educational work in India known in such a way as to attract the most desirable candidates? Unless an affirmative answer can confidently be given to both these questions, it is statesmanship itself which is at fault, not the educational services. They are what Government has made them. But this is not all. Of all the great work done in India during the last hundred years, there has been none more difficult to do than the work of higher education. "High class education has much to struggle against in this country," wrote the second Director of Public Instruction in the Bombay Presidency in 1860, and it is still true in 1911. The task taken in hand was, indeed, incredible, the difficulties almost insuperable, so much so that critics, not ill-qualified, now declare the whole movement to have been a mistake; not observing, as I think, the great advance, intellectual and moral, made between 1835 and 1910. Let a little more credit be given to the men who have struggled against these difficulties and worked on quietly and unostentatiously in a sphere of labour withdrawn from the the main current of official preferment. At least, let the Indian public acknowledge what it owes to those by whose labour and devotion the educational system has been built up, and by renewed efforts brought nearer to thoroughness and efficiency. This is said for the men of the higher educational service first, because in them is vested a certain primacy in virtue of the qualifications demanded of them and of their relation to Government. But it is said also for all classes of educational workers: for the Provincial Service, for the Subordinate and Lower Subordinate Services, all in their places and degrees, and for the numerous workers of all grades outside Government service in missionary and private institutions; for all who have done and are doing faithful educational service of any kind. Very much more might be said: this much perhaps suffices for the purpose of these papers.

XV

THE POLITICAL MOVEMENT IN ITS RELATION TO EDUCATION

The life of a community cannot be separated into unrelated compartments any more than the life of an individual. Each part affects the rest. The development of one faculty, or side of character, produces effects on other faculties, and influences the organism as a whole. And so the educational movement has, in a certain sense, been political from the outset. That is to say, in the very nature of things, and by reason of the essential constitution of the mind, it was impossible to educate a single native of India without thereby affecting his relation to British rule. Education enables a man to understand better society, government, and his own relation to both. An educated man is able to place himself in the universe; to realize better his true relation to what has gone before, and what will come after. If political ideas are in the air, the educated man will make acquaintance with them, and they will alter his mental outlook. So it might have been predicted, and so it was.

Raja Ram Mohan Roy was, I suppose, the first English educated native of India. He reached man's estate about the year 1802; and there was nothing that could be called English education publicly begun till 1817. He owed his education and his knowledge of English to his own genius and exertions. He was no enemy to British rule, though he relates in his brief autobiography that he began "with a great aversion to the establishment of the British power in India." It was after he was twenty years of age that he first "saw and began to associate with Europeans," and soon after, he says, "made myself tolerably acquainted with their laws and form of government!" He continues: "Finding them generally more intelligent, more steady and moderate in their conduct, I gave up my prejudice against them, and became inclined in their favour, *feeling persuaded that their rule, though a foreign yoke, would lead more speedily and surely to the amelioration of the native inhabitants*; and I enjoyed the confidence of several of them, even in their public capacity." This, on a fair view, is typical of the normal effects of education in the general. That the natives of India, Hindu or Mahomedan, Mahratta or Madrasi, should naturally and spontaneously prefer a foreign government and admire manners and customs so unlike their own is altogether against nature. To suppose that antipathy to European ways, and criticism of European manners are new, and the pernicious effects of "English education," is to be ignorant alike of the laws of human nature and the plain facts of history. The natural and "unenlightened" view of English manners and customs has been vividly drawn by Trevelyan in his "Competition Wallah":—

"But, on the other hand, many of our usages must, in their eyes, appear most debased and revolting. Imagine the horror with which a punctilious and devout Brahmin cannot but regard a people who eat the flesh of cows and pigs, and drink various sorts of strong liquor from morning till night. It is at least as hard for such a man to look up to us as his betters, morally and socially, as it would be for us to place amongst the most civilized nations of the world a population which was in the habit of dining on human flesh, and intoxicating itself daily with laudanum and sal-volatile."[1] This is from the natural standpoint of Hindu orthodoxy, and the effect of education could hardly be to deepen such aversion. It might do something to temper it.

Neither is criticism of the British Government really anything new. Before the close of the eighteenth century, when the British administration of Bengal was still a novelty not twenty years old, Syed Gholam Hossein Khan, in the fourteenth section of his *Seir Mutakherin*, or "Review of Modern Times," is at pains to set forth at length twelve causes of the decrease of population and revenue which he laments. The first is "that these new rulers are quite alien to this country both in customs and manners"; the second "their differing in language, as well as in almost every action and every custom in life." And yet the Syed is in many respects an admirer and shows readiness to accord praise to the forceful foreigners, when in his judgment it is due. Some of his "causes," curiously enough, such as inaccessibility to interviewers, frequent changes of appointments, excessive regard for promotion by seniority, are the commonplaces of criticism of the Anglo-Indian bureaucracy to this day. He even gives a large place in his sixth cause to the "drain." "The sixth cause is that the English have deprived the inhabitants of these countries of various branches of commerce and benefit, which they had ever enjoyed heretofore." Similarly, Ram Mohan Roy, in his evidence to the Select Committee of the House of Commons, which was considering the renewal of the Company's charter in 1831, refers to the

[1] *Trevelyan* (Sir George Otto), "The Competition Wallah" (Macmillan), 2nd ed., p. 346.

"large sum of money now annually drawn from India by Europeans retiring from it with the fortunes realized there." There is really not very much difference in the point of view of Syed Gholam Hossein Khan writing about 1780, Ram Mohan Roy writing in 1831, and Mr. Romesh Chunder Dutt writing in 1901, though the first knew little or no English, the second was educated before Government introduced any system of education, and the third is the fine flower of English education. The truth is that the criticism, sound or unsound, arises out of the circumstances,[1] and would be in the minds of the peoples of India, altogether independently of their power of expressing it in English. All three may be said to be well affected towards British rule in the sense of willing it to continue.

If we inquire into the causes of disaffection, it may plausibly be suggested that we shall find them to depend little on education, at least directly; indirectly they may depend a good deal. Disaffection is the contrary of affection. In the mildest degree it connotes merely the absence of affection, and passes from this through every degree of dislike up to settled hatred. Education has certainly not produced in India hatred of all things English; not obviously of English literature, English games, English standards of conduct, English institutions: because the political party which voices the aspirations of the educated classes in India, and is

[1] On the vexed question of "the drain," the fair-minded inquirer should read chaps. viii. and ix. of Sir Theodore Morison's recently-published book "The Economic Transition in India." See especially p. 241: "The answer, then, which I give to the question, 'What economic equivalent does India get for foreign payments?' is this: India gets the equipment of modern industry, and she gets an administration favourable to economic evolution cheaper than she could provide it herself."

charged with being disaffected, or allied with disaffection, is founded on an almost servile imitation of English standards and methods. As regards forms of government, it probably holds that men everywhere are well affected towards a government which they clearly see secures their welfare. Habit and sentiment are powerful adjuncts. A government is strong when it appeals to the national sentiment, and suits the traditional habits of the people who dwell under it. These latter supports have, from the circumstances, been almost wholly denied to the British Government in India. It was certainly so a hundred years ago, and it is doubtful whether these forces have as yet been very successfully rallied to it. That they might conceivably be rallied to it has not been beyond the pitch of a few daring speculators like Sir Theodore Morison.[1] The support of the interest of the people at large it has had, and the clearest thinkers believe it has now in an even greater degree. It may be asked whether education is or is not likely to produce in men's minds a perception of their true interests. If, as must almost certainly be answered, it does tend to produce such a perception, the Government of India may be reasonably assured (superficial appearances to the contrary notwithstanding) of gaining strength from the spread of education, so long as it does really what it claims to do, secure the best interests of the Indian peoples. This, it may still be believed, has on the whole been the effect of the spread of education in British India.

One of the questions answered by Raja Ram Mohan Roy in 1831 was, "What is the prevailing opinion of the native inhabitants regarding the existing form of government and its administrators, native and European?"

[1] "Imperial Rule in India," chap. x., cf. chap. iv.

His answer has interest, and even some relevance, to-day: "The peasantry and villagers in the interior," he wrote, "are quite ignorant of, and indifferent about, either the former or present government, and attribute the protection they may enjoy, or oppression they may suffer, to the conduct of the public officers immediately presiding over them. But men of aspiring character, and members of such families as are very much reduced by the present system, consider it derogatory to accept of the trifling public situations which natives are allowed to hold under the British Government, and are decidedly disaffected to it. Many of those, however, who engage prosperously in commerce, and of those who are secured in the peaceful possession of their estates by the permanent settlement, and such as have sufficient intelligence to foresee the probability of future improvement, which presents itself under the British rulers, are not only reconciled to it, but really view it as a blessing to the country." And then he concludes: "But I have no hesitation in stating, with reference to the general feeling of the more intelligent part of the native community, that *the only course of policy which can ensure their attachment to any form of Government would be that of making them eligible to gradual promotion according to their respective abilities and merits, to situations of trust and respectability in the State.*" Now these concluding words express with very fair exactness what has actually been both the aim and the outcome of the whole movement for education, seen on its political side. We may make again, now, the claim which the Commission of 1882 made in reporting on the effects of higher education, "An estimate of the effect which collegiate instruction has had upon the general education and enlightenment of the people *must in fairness be accompanied by a reference to the objects which it sets before itself.*" Now, what were these objects? They reached, no doubt, to general moral and intellectual enlightenment; but they were also expressly directed to the well-defined and limited object of fitting men by education for the public service. Thus, a letter from the Court of Directors, dated September 5th, 1827 (eight years, be it noticed, before Macaulay's Minute), has these words: "In conclusion it is proper to remark to you, though we have no doubt that the same reflection has already occurred to you, that, adverting to the daily increasing demand for the employment of natives in the business of the country, and in important departments of the Government, the first object of improved education should be to prepare a body of individuals for discharging public duties. It may, we trust, be expected that the intended course of education will not only produce a higher degree of intellectual fitness, but that it will contribute to raise the moral character of those who partake of its advantages, and supply you with servants to whose probity you may, with increased confidence, commit offices of trust. To this, the last and highest object of education, we expect that a large share of your attention will be applied." Sir Charles Trevelyan, writing in 1838, says: "Another great change has of late years been made in our Indian administration, which ought alone to excite us to corresponding exertions for the education of the natives. The system established by Lord Cornwallis was based upon the principle of doing everything by European agency. . . . The plan which Lord William Bentinck substituted for it was to transact the public business by native agency, under European superintendence, and this change is now in progress in all the different branches of administration. We have already native judges, collectors, and opium and salt agents; and it is now proposed to have native magistrates. . . . The success of this great measure depends entirely on the fitness of the natives for the exercise of the new functions to which they have been called."[1] In 1844 came Lord Hardinge's resolution, raising selection for employment under Government on educational grounds into a recognized principle. The Despatch of 1854, besides referring back in one of its opening paragraphs to the letter of September, 1827, and later on to the resolution of 1844, definitely puts increased fitness for employment in the public services as one of the chief aims of the educational system to be inaugurated: "We have always been of opinion that the spread of education in India will produce a greater efficiency in all branches of administration, by enabling you to obtain the services of intelligent and trustworthy persons in every department of Government, and, on the other hand, we believe that the numerous vacancies of different kinds, which have constantly to be filled up, may afford a great stimulus to education." Further, the Despatch claims that a measure of success has already been won: "We are sanguine enough to believe that some effect has already been produced by the improved education of the public service of India. The ability and integrity of a large and increasing number of the native judges, to whom the greater part of the civil jurisdiction in India is now committed, and the high estimation in which many among them are held by their fellow-countrymen, is, in our opinion, much to be attributed to the progress of education among these officers, and to their adoption, along with it, of that high moral tone which pervades

[1] Trevelyan (Sir Charles), "On the Education of the People in India," p. 156.

the general literature of Europe." This judgment is re-affirmed by the Commission of 1882, with stronger assurance. After the words already quoted, the report continues: "The reformers of 1835, to whom the system is due, claimed that only by an education in English and after European methods could we hope to raise the moral and intellectual tone of Indian society, and supply the administration with a competent body of public servants. To what degree, then, have these objects been attained? Our answer is in the testimony of witnesses before this Commission, in the thoughtful opinion delivered from time to time by men whose position has given them ample opportunities of judging, and the facts obvious to all eyes throughout the country, and that answer is conclusive; if not that collegiate education has fulfilled all the expectations entertained of it, at least that it has not disappointed the hopes of a sober judgment." This was in 1883. It remains to consider whether, on a careful balance, the same verdict may not be pronounced in 1911.

The process so well known to us all, to which the quotations above refer, namely, the substitution of Indian for European agency in higher and ever higher positions of responsibility, has gone on continuously since 1883, sometimes with increasing momentum, and so far the favourable verdict has not been reversed. The consummation, the legitimate consummation, the consummation which was deliberately aimed at from the beginning, is the reformed Councils and the eloquent speeches of the leaders of Indian opinion, which we read daily when the Imperial and Provincial Councils are in session. The aims which are now being realized are, perhaps, even better expressed by statesmen of the type of Mountstuart Elphinstone and Sir Thomas Munro than by the public documents which have been quoted. In 1826 Elphinstone wrote in a private letter: "It has always been a favourite notion of mine that our object ought to be to place ourselves in the same relation to the natives as the Tartars are in to the Chinese; retaining the government and military power, but gradually relinquishing all share in the civil administration, except that degree of control which is necessary to give the whole an impulse and direction. This operation must be so gradual that it need not even alarm the directors for their civil patronage; but it ought to be kept in mind, and all our measures ought to tend to that object. The first steps are to commence a systematic education of the natives for civil offices, to make over to them at once a larger share of judicial business, to increase their emoluments generally, and to open a few high prizes for the most able and honest among them. The period when they may be admitted into Council (as you propose) seems to be distant. . . ."[1] To Sir Thomas Munro he had written in 1822: "Besides the necessity for having good native advisers in governing natives, it is necessary that we should pave the way for the introduction of the natives to some share in the government of their own country. It may be half a century before we are obliged to do so; but the system of Government and of education which we have already established must some time or other work such a change on the people of this country, that it will be impossible to confine them to subordinate employments. . . ."[2] Of Sir Thomas Munro his biographer, Sir Alexander Arbuthnot, writes: "Munro attached little value to schemes for improving the education of natives unless *pari passu* steps were taken for extending to them a

[1] Colebrooke: "Life of Mountstuart Elphinstone, vol. ii., p. 186.
[2] Ib., vol. ii., p. 143.

greater share in the honours and emoluments of office. His view was that the two things, education and higher employment, should go together."[1] The inner significance of the whole process was expressed in 1821 by Sir Thomas Munro himself with a force and truth which could not be surpassed: "Our present system of Government by excluding all natives from power and trust and emolument is much more efficacious in depressing than all our laws and school-books can do in elevating their character. We are working against our own designs, and we can expect to make no progress while we work with a feeble instrument to improve and a powerful one to deteriorate. The improvement of the character of a people and the keeping them at the same time in the lowest state of dependency on foreign rulers to which they can be reduced by conquest, are matters quite incompatible with each other."[2] Again he wrote in 1824: "No conceit more wild and absurd than this was ever engendered in the darkest ages; for what is in every age and every country the great stimulus to the pursuit of knowledge, but the prospect of fame, or wealth, or power? Or what is even the use of great attainments, if they are not to be devoted to their noblest purpose, the service of the community, by employing those who possess them, according to their respective qualifications, in the various duties of the public administration of the country."[3] The very oddity and irrelevance of these quotations now is a measure of the distance travelled since 1820. It is not amiss that these earlier forms of thought should be called to mind for those, on the one hand, who are apt to ignore what advance has been made in admitting educated

[1] Arbuthnot, "Major General Sir Thomas Munro," p. 154.
[2] Ib., p. 148.
[3] Ib., p. 150.

Indians to posts of high responsibility and for those on the other who are ignorant of the great results which higher education has actually achieved. Even Lord Morley himself misses this, when the best he can find to say for higher education in India is that it has not wholly failed.[1] Not only has higher education not failed to achieve what in 1835 it set out to do, but it has triumphantly succeeded; perhaps it has even succeeded too well. For though its success in training well-qualified candidates for public service is the most direct fulfilment of the original aim and purpose, it is by no means the whole achievement, or even the greatest part of it. Trevelyan writes in the monograph: "On the education of the People of India," from which quotation has already been made: "The same means which will secure for the Government a body of intelligent and upright native servants will stimulate the mental activity and improve the morals of the people at large. The Government cannot make public employment the reward of distinguished merit without encouraging merit in all who look forward to public employ; it cannot open schools for educating its servants, without diffusing knowledge among all classes of its subjects."[2] These predictions also have been abundantly fulfilled. The renewed productivity of half a dozen literatures, the revival of art and letters, alert and critical interest in the past history and literature of Indian races (voiced as it was, for instance, eloquently but with unflinching recognition of present "shortcomings," by Dr. Ashutosh Mukhopadhyaya, Vice-Chancellor of Calcutta University, at this year's Convocation) bear witness to the stimulation of mental activity.

[1] "British Democracy and Indian Government," by the Right Hon. Viscount Morley, O.M. *Nineteenth Century* for February, 1911, p. 209.

[2] "On the Education of the People of India," p. 159.

K

The capacity for combination shown by numerous associations for social, literary and recreative purposes is a moral endowment. All these new capacities and powers education has conferred on the classes who have been able to profit by it. The bounds of legitimate aspiration are also herein clearly settled. This education was instituted by the British Government to enable the peoples of India to take a larger and more important *share* in the work of administration. This larger share of responsibility and employment has been accorded to them. The process is in mid-career. That there should be differences of opinion as to the ultimate limits of the process and as to the extent which is the due limit at any given time, is only natural. The aspiration for a larger share than that already gained is perfectly legitimate, and Indians may combine to secure this larger share by constitutional means: it is equally legitimate to hold the contrary view and oppose further extension. The bounds of legitimate aspiration are the limits consistent with the stability of British rule.

But what then of the bugbear of anarchism and unrest? Measured by this standard it shrinks marvellously. These intellectual and moral results are the direct product of higher education; discontent and conspiracy, if to be called products of education at all, are indirect products, like some harmful bi-product of a useful chemical process. The causes of unrest in the sinister sense are foreign domination, racial prejudice, ignorance, misunderstanding, narrowness, want of education, lack of sympathy. Education is not directly a cause at all: indirectly it may, perhaps, be called a cause as putting these latent forces into activity. Education could never in any sound sense of the term lead to anarchist crime. A depraved and perverted nature may use the powers that education gives to evil purpose. A radically unsound education might help to produce criminals, but even so it must rather be from failure to supply deterrents than from positively supplying incentives. The education being given in Indian schools and colleges only contributes to the morbid condition of things that has produced political conspiracy and crime by its defects, by its unwholesome surroundings, by its failure to educate in any true sense at all. For want of foresight in allowing education to spread beyond the limits of effective control those in various degrees responsible for its organization must bear the blame. But the education itself must not be blamed: only the failure to make it effective. For the direct purpose of education in primary schools, in secondary schools, and in colleges alike, has been to train the will in obedience and in good habits, as well as to train the intellect. So far as the schools and colleges have failed in this, the purpose of education has been missed. All violence and breach of law are contrary to the very idea of education. The higher the education the greater the incompatibility of its influences with cruelty, treachery, physical violence and secret murder. Enlightenment must and does hate these things, and must still do so, even if it proclaimed the ultimate right of insurrection for national freedom. But in India enlightenment cannot proclaim the right of insurrection at all. For that enlightenment itself comes from the central power which holds together the congeries of races and creeds and peoples which make up modern India and alone gives unity alike to education and to political aspiration. The aim to destroy that central power would be not murder only but suicide as well. Success in that aim would inevitably throw back all the advance towards liberty made in the last hundred years, to which even the revolutionary aim itself owes such life and power as it has. It is just because all hopes of peaceful development and prosperity really are bound up with the maintenance of the one strong and stable government, that education must in proportion as it is true and thorough strengthen the forces that make for cohesion, not for disruption. The greater the independence of judgment, the deeper the insight that education gives, the clearer must be the perception of these truths.

It is not meant in anything that has been said to question that the political developments of the last twenty years have given grave cause for anxiety and that their association with higher education in any sense is deeply to be regretted. We can no longer speak with the confidence of Sir Roper Lethbridge in defending "High Education in India" in 1882, when he wrote: "And for contradiction of the vague and unauthenticated aspersions on the character of the highly-educated section of the Indian community for loyalty, for morality, for religion generally, we need only look to the tone and character of that portion of the periodical press that is conducted and written by such men." This we certainly can no longer say: but here in the rapid depravation of an uncontrolled press, we have (as I think Mr. Chirol himself shows) the real propagating agency of the gathering mischief, and not in education: and the regulation of the press, now that it has been firmly taken in hand, is already working a remedy.

XVI

CONCLUSIONS

THE endeavour has now been made to follow the history of the educational system established in India from its beginnings and the verdict on the whole, with plain and specific deductions, is favourable. At every critical stage weight has been given to opposing considerations and the conclusion at every stage is that practically no other course was possible than that which was taken. When enlightened Bengali gentlemen started the Hindu College and a little later on asked for the help and support of Government, Government did rightly in giving the financial aid asked for and could not consistently with its position and responsibilities have done otherwise. When the question was raised whether it was more expedient for higher education that the study of English should be encouraged or whether State aid should be confined to Arabic and Sanskrit, the decision given in 1835 in favour of English was the right decision. When twenty-two years later universities were founded, though plausible reasons were given at the time for considering such a high enterprise premature, the practical economic success of the universities and the effects produced intellectually and morally in the course of a generation prove that the fears expressed before 1857 were mistaken, that universities met a real want and that the progress attained justified their institution. A more doubtful judgment must be passed on the adoption of one of the recommendations of the Commission of 1882, that, namely, for the withdrawal of Government from the direct control of higher education: but as that has been materially modified since, especially by the operation of the Universities Act of 1904, less need be said about the error. Well-intentioned as was the recommendation to encourage educational progress mainly through grants-in-aid, the actual result undoubtedly was to bring into existence numbers of institutions imperfectly staffed, equipped and financed, with the further result of a tendency to pull down educational standards. Effort has been made in the years since 1901 to correct this tendency. The complaint that moral and religious education has been neglected is partly unjustified by the facts, because it has from the first been a part of the educational aim to train character as well as to impart knowledge, and further Government has not failed to call special attention to the importance of this side of education. It is partly due to misapprehension of the circumstances and failure to recognize the inevitable limitations imposed by the conditions under which the work of education in India is carried on.

The grand charge against education now is that the system as a whole is mainly responsible for the embitterment of political feeling in recent years and for the rancorous expression of disaffection in speech and writing: finally that the responsibility for revolutionary crimes is to be added to the account. Reason has been shown for thinking this charge to be grossly misstated and in this unqualified form inadmissible. Political disaffection is due to political causes, not primarily to education. There is confusion between disaffection and the effective expression of disaffection. Education enables the disaffected to express themselves more effectively, but it is not except in a minor degree itself a cause of disaffection. Revolutionary crime has been recklessly ascribed to the "student class"; but this is a very loose and careless ascription. If inquiry be made into the histories and antecedents of youths who have figured as the leading actors in the wretched conspiracies and outrages which have troubled the peace of the two Bengals and of Bombay, it will be found that only a small proportion of them are to be characterized as "students" in the sense ordinarily recognized by those connected with education. Students in the strict sense are undergraduates who have passed the Matriculation examination of one of the universities and are actually studying in some affiliated college. The name may with some propriety be extended to include boys in the upper classes of high schools who are undergoing a training which leads to university study. Not every youth who has been to school and knows a little English is to be reckoned a student, nor should the evil doings of young men who draw ill lessons from mis-study of the *Gita* be put to the account of English education. A great wrong has in public opinion been done in this matter. The great body of students, whatever the precise temperature of their loyalty, and whatever their occasional readiness to flock to listen to public speakers of repute, are neither revolutionaries, nor conspirators; nor are colleges hotbeds of sedition, unless the frequent absence of a warm affection for English things and persons and a weak tendency to compare Western "materialism" to its disadvantage with the assumed "spirituality" of the East merit such a designation. So far as I know, not a single trained chemist has had a hand in the manufacture of a bomb; nor are the leaders of fancy dacoit bands men who have won scholarships, or who aspire to university Honours. No, the whole force of real education is opposed to violence and crooked methods. Culture —and after all education in India aims at culture—as Matthew Arnold says, "hates hatred; culture has but one great passion, the passion for sweetness and light."

It is not true, then, it cannot be true, that education, the cultivation of intellectual excellence and the endeavour to give efficacy in conduct to the highest motives, tends in India to produce virulent enemies of a just and righteous administration, still less reckless fanatics, ripe for any crime in the name of revolution. If there is any truth at all in the ascription of some hurtful effects to the educational system in working, it is true only in a carefully qualified sense and in strictness due not to education, but to defect of education. Yet even were the charge truer than it is, education must go on, because (as all agree) it cannot now be stopped; and must go on mainly on the lines already laid; so that the practical problem would be how to make the best of it; not how to change it radically, but how to remove imperfections, amend and strengthen. The moral in the end is that the effort to promote the true ends of education must not be slackened, but redoubled. The remedy lies not in coming to a stop and beginning again, but in steady and more careful advance on the lines laid. In one sense a new departure is called for. Such a putting forth of effort is required as would practically raise the whole work of education to a higher plane. Aims and motives have not been high enough, not sincere enough, not thorough enough. In particular is this true of the side of education which touches character.

For there are, on the other hand, very manifest imperfections, which incidentally this inquiry has brought out, in the system of education as it now is; imperfections which may be remedied and which it should be the business of statesmanship to remedy as far as carefully thought out measures can find remedy.

First and most important is the strengthening of the moral side of education in colleges and schools. Moral education has not been overlooked. It has been the direct concern of Government policy all along, and it has latterly exercised the anxious thought of all taking part in the work of education. Yet certainly enough has not been done. For this the surpassing difficulties of the task attempted is very largely responsible. But along with that, and all the more because of that, it must be realized that the attempt has failed partly because it has been made on too low a plane. The potent aid of religion is denied as we have concluded, in Indian education. But the moral relations themselves are sacred and the teacher's calling is a sacred calling. Have we made all that is possible of positive duty, of the personal influence of the teacher, of the restraints and impulses of school and college discipline? The well-organized college or school, that image of a state in miniature, founded as it should be in righteousness, regulated in all its parts for the general good and the attainment of high ends outside self, is a capital instrument of moral education. Loyalty to the teacher, loyalty to the school, loyalty to the college, these are motive forces with great potency for moulding and strengthening character, if rightly wielded.

Secondly, it is clear from what has just been said, that only through the personal influence of the teacher can these great moral results be attained. A high moral tone cannot be communicated to an institution by any rescript, decree or ordinance of State. Rightly devised rules of life will do a great deal, but even these must be informed by the right spirit; a mere lifeless conformity will effect little; even the conformity is sure to be lax without a desire to conform. The right spirit must grow up among the body of students and can be communicated, so far as it is capable of communication, only by the teachers. So the ideals of the teachers and the faithfulness with which they live by them are the real source of moral vitality in school and college.

But how, thirdly, in soberness can the policy of the State affect the ideals of teachers appointed for work in schools and colleges? Is not this to ask something that belongs to quite a different category from departmental machinery? It might be asked in reply what effort has ever been made to raise the men engaged in England for educational work in India to a consciousness of the greatness of the task to which they are invited and the character of the responsibilities to be laid upon them. Is any history of that work, any account of its claims and opportunities and difficulties, ever put before applicants? This might at least be considered before it is concluded that all that is possible has been done towards securing the right attitude of mind in the men brought by the State to India to take the lead in educational work.

In India still more, fourthly, might a genuine desire to raise the status of the teacher manifest itself actively. It may seem inconsistent to talk of emoluments and prospects, when the question is of ideals and character. Yet emoluments and status are certainly closely connected in India (perhaps even more than in other countries) and it might be well on grounds other than commercial to improve the emoluments and prospects of all classes of educational workers. Is the status of the teacher satisfactory now? For answer consult heads of colleges and professors, headmasters and inspectors of schools, as to the social recognition publicly accorded to them. Indian dutifulness once held teachers venerable and worthy of the highest respect. Does it do so now? There is room for amendment both of State policy and public demeanour in this matter; and amendment in this matter would strengthen the hands of teachers for the work they are told to do.

Fifthly, another direction in which we may look with great hopefulness is the development of college and school as institutions. When fully developed the sentiment called forth by the institution may be even more powerful in its sway over conduct than the influence of individual teachers. Here a departmental system is to some extent a hindrance, because to a department a college or school is necessarily not a self-contained whole, but one member of a group. Recent tendencies, however, have all been in the direction of giving fuller recognition to the organic unity of the institution and a measure of autonomy is already attained by the colleges within the bounds of the department. It is on this ground as well as on the ground that students living uncared for and insufficiently supervised in "messes" are exposed to dangers, physical and moral, that the immediate prospect of a large provision of hostels in Calcutta is so greatly a matter of congratulation. In order that the full benefit may be realized, it is essential that this provision of hostels should be based on the unity of the college as an institution. This is indeed part of the ideal of the complete residential college, now fully accepted by the University. The members of the college not only study in the same class rooms, but share a social life which extends to all three sides of education, intellectual, physical and moral.

Lastly, the greatest need and the greatest hope for higher education in a broad sense lies in a recognition in the near future of the comparative neglect from which school education has long suffered and the adoption of a systematic policy of giving the schools their rightful place in national education. The hopefulness consists in this, that so much more can be done with school-boys. The habits, intellectual and moral, formed in the earlier years count more than later influences. If the schools lay the foundations of character and intellectual life wrongly, hardly can four or even six years at college repair the mischief; but if the schools do their work adequately and well, the chief obstacles in the way of success in college education will have been cleared away.

The whole problem of education in India is so vast that only some of its aspects have been treated in these papers, and that cursorily. On the main question, I venture to think the answer is complete. The work of Government and of the Education departments is vindicated. This vindication holds as against the impatience of advanced political thinkers who complain that too little has been done and grasp at a hasty realization of the ends towards which the educational process is working before the work of training is sufficiently advanced; and also against the one-sided condemnation of critics who pay disproportionate attention to the morbid products of a vast intellectual and moral transmutation and decline to see to what extent these are merely incidental to a process in itself essentially healthy and beneficial. It appears that the policy of the Government of India from the beginning of the nineteenth century to the present day has in the main been justified by its results as well as in its inception; that no startling reversal of policy is called for, not even any radical change in the direction of its leading activities. Improvement in the details, expansion all along the line, more liberal employment of funds, these are wanted, as they always have been wanted. For the rest, the watchword is "Forward" and not "Back"; "Courage" and not words of doubt and despondency. The movement is greater than the men who have taken part in it. Individuals may doubt and repine at what has been done in their name and by their means. But this work of education *is* the work of the British in India. The spirit of it is in the race and works in spite of the individuals who do not understand it and cavil at it. It has spoken out from time to time in the words of some master mind, and stands recorded in the great public documents which express the avowed policy of the State.

BIBLIOGRAPHY.

Trevelyan (Sir Charles Edward). On the Education of the People of India. Longman, Orme, Brown, Green & Longmans. 1838.

Kerr (James). A Review of Public Instruction in the Bengal Presidency. W. H. Allen. 1853.

Howell (Arthur). Education in British India. Calcutta. 1872.

Lethbridge (Sir Roper). High Education in India. W. H. Allen & Co. 1882.

Mahmood (Syed). A History of English Education in India (1781 to 1893). Aligarh. 1895.

Satthianadhan. History of Education in the Madras Presidency. Srinivasa, Varadachari & Co. Madras. 1894.

Reports of Public Instruction in Bengal from 1831.

Minutes of the Calcutta University from 1857.

Quinquennial Reviews of the Progress of Education in India from 1886.

Educational Despatch of 1854.

Report of the Education Commission of 1882.

Report of the Universities Commission of 1902.

Resolution of the Government of India, March, 1904.

Colebrooke (Sir T. E.). Life of the Honourable Mountstuart Elphinstone. 2 vols. Murray. 1884.

Arbuthnot (Sir A. J.). Life of Major-General Sir Thomas Munro. Kegan Paul, Trench & Co. 1889.

Morison (Sir Theodore). Imperial Rule in India. Constable. 1899.

Craik (Sir Henry). Impressions of India. Macmillan. 1908.

Mitra (S. C.). Indian Problems. Murray. 1908.

Arbuthnot (Sir A. J.). Memories of Rugby and India. Fisher Unwin. 1910.

Chirol (Valentine). Indian Unrest. Macmillan. 1910.

Morison (Sir Theodore). The Economic Transition in India. Murray. 1911.

PRINTED BY WILLIAM CLOWES AND SONS, LIMITED, LONDON AND BECCLES.